Sri:
Srimathe Ramanujaya Nama:

Statements of Thirukkolur Ammal
Thirukkolur Ammal Varththaigal
(Thirukkolur Penpillai Rahasyam)

Author: TCA Venkatesan

Azhvar Emberumanar Jeeyar Thiruvadigale Sharanam

Statements of Thirukkolur Ammal by TCA Venkatesan
Published by Amazon Kindle Direct Publishing

Copyright © 2019 by TCA Venkatesan

All rights reserved. No part of this publication may be reproduced, distributed, or transmitted in any form or by any means, including photocopying, recording, or other electronic or mechanical methods, without the prior written permission of the publisher, except in the case of brief quotations embodied in critical reviews and certain other noncommercial uses permitted by copyright law.

Printed in the United States of America

First Printing, 2019

Ebook ASIN: B07Z3WYQYT
https://www.amazon.com/dp/B07Z3WYQYT

Printed Book ISBN: 9781701204195 / ASIN: 1701204193
https://www.amazon.com/dp/1701204193

Cover Design: Amazon Kindle Direct Publishing

Thirukkolur Ammal Vaarththaigal

Foreword

This is a list of rhetorical questions asked by a lady called Thirukkolour Ammal to Bhagavad Ramanuja in the outskirts of a divyadesam in southern Tamilnadu called Thirukkolur. Thirukkolur is the birthplace of Madhurakavi Azhvar.

She has expressed her naichyam (lowliness) through these statements. This naichya bhavam is required of all Srivaishnavas as they strive to be of service, without the thought that they are superior to anyone. With these statements, she has also brought forth many beautiful events from Sri Ramayanam, Mahabharatam and the lives of the great Srivaishnava acharyas.

This book is based on the work of Dr V V Ramanujam written in Tamil. The images used in this book are from the author's personal collection and low resolution, sample images from the internet. All rights to the full images belong to the creator.

The author expresses his gratitude to Dr V V Ramanujam Swami and the scholars who have explained the meanings of these statements and the Srivaishnava acharyas who recorded and transmitted these noble messages for everyones benefit.

Thirukkolur Ammal Vaarththaigal

Avatharikai

One time Swami Ramanuja was going to Thirukkolur, a divyadesam in southern Tamilnadu, India. In the outskirts of the divyadesam, a lady came and bowed to him.

Swami Ramanuja asked her "Where are you coming from?"

She replied that she was coming out of Thirukkolur. Upon hearing it, Ramanuja said "Sharing one person's cloth between seven people and eating anything - that is even with great struggle, everyone tries to enter Thirukkolur. This is mentioned by Nammazhvar as *'thiNNam en iLamAn pugum Ur thirukkOLUrE'*, in his Thiruvaymozhi. How is it that for you, this is a place to leave?"

The lady replied "*adiyEn! nAyanthE nAyanthE!*" and gave the 81 statements that are collectively called as *'Thirukkolur Ammal Vaarththaigal'*.

She continued "If I had the same knowledge as those mentioned in the 81 statements, then I could stay in Thirukkolur. I do not possess that. Does it matter if a rabbit's droppings were in the field or on the wayside?"

She then requested Ramanuja "If you were to visit Thirukkolur, then all the festivals of Vaiththamanidhi Perumal and Madhurakavi Azhvar would occur grandly".

Hearing her words, Ramanujar was pleased, visited her home, asked her to cook a meal and ate it (normally this would not be done by a sanyasi). He then gave her prasadam and holy water.

This event was mentioned by Periya Vanamamalai Jeeyar, having heard it from Thiruvaymozhippillai.

Vaarththai 1

1. azhaiththu varugiREn enREnO akrUraraip pOlE

க. அழைத்து வருகிறேன் என்றேனோ அக்ரூரரைப் போலே

Kamsa had tried to kill Sri Krishna several times as he was growing up in Gokulam. Failing in these attempts, he decided to try to get Him and Sri Balarama to come to Mathura and try to kill them there. So, he organized a bow festival ('*viRperu vizhavu*') and sent an invitation to them both through Akrura, who was a Yadava and a close relative to Vasudeva. His plan was to kill them through his royal elephant Kuvalayapeedam or through his royal wrestlers Chanura and Mushtika.

The wise Akrura had great love for Krishna and knew that He was none other than Sriman Narayana. Thus, he knew that Kamsa's plan would not work. However, wishing to see Krishna and enjoy His presence, he agreed to be the messenger for Kamsa and went to get Krishna and Balarama.

All along the way, he thought of nothing but Krishna and being in His company. He then met Krishna and Balarama and brought them back with him to Mathura in his chariot. Thus he gained Krishna's grace.

Thirukkolur Ammal is saying "Did I or can I do what Akrura did".

Vaarththai 2

2. agamozhiththu viTTEnO vidhuraraip pOlE

உ. அகமொழித்து விட்டேனோ விதுரரைப் போலே

Vidhura was the brother and advisor of King Drudrirashtra. He was very wise and had great devotion to Sri Krishna.

When, at the end of the thirteen years of leaving their kingdom, the Pandavas asked for it back, Duryodhana refused. To avoid war, Krishna went as a messenger of the Pandavas to the Kauravas, to their capital Hastinapura.

At Hastinapura, Krishna did not wish to go and stay at Duryodhana's palace or those of his near ones. Instead, He went to Vidhura's home, even though it was a small place compared to the palaces of the Kauravas. Vidhura became extremely happy at seeing Krishna. He entertained Him to the best of his abilities and thus expressed his great love for Krishna. Krishna too accepted whatever Vidhura gave, because it was given without a selfish reason and offered with great devotion.

Thirukkolur Ammal is saying "Can I show the selfless love and value that Vidhura exhibited", or she is saying "Can I give my heart completely to Krishna, like Vidhura did".

Vaarththai 3

3. dhEhaththai viTTEnO rushi pathniyaip pOlE

௩. தேஹத்தை விட்டேனோ ருஷி பத்னியைப் போலே

One time Krishna, Balarama and the yadava kids took their cows into the forest for grazing. There they rested and ate the food that they had brought along. Even after eating everything that they had, they remained hungry. So, the children asked Krishna to help them get more food.

In a nearby area, several Brahmins (refered here as Rishis) were performing a yAga. Krishna asked the yadavas to go and tell them "Krishna is nearby, He is hungry and is asking for food". But when the yadavas went and asked the Brahmins, they kept quiet and ignored them. The children became sad, came back to Krishna and told Him what happened.

Hearing that, Krishna pointed out the wives of the Brahmins to the yadavas and told them "Go to them and tell that Krishna and Balarama are hungry and are asking for food".

When the ladies heard this, they became anxious to see Krishna and Balarama and came to them with different types of food. The did this in spite of the fact that the Brahmins forbade them from doing so. Krishna accepted the food and told them "Please go back to your husbands and help them complete their yAga. Do not be afraid. They will take you back".

The women then went back to their husbands. One of the brahmins, however, refused to take his wife back. At that point, keeping Krishna in her heart, she sacrificed her body.

The brahmins then realized their mistake and surrendered to Krishna. The place where Krishna sat waiting for food is called Baddhavilochanam (*Nachchiyar Thirumozhi* 12-6).

Thirukkolur Ammal says "Am I capable of being like the rishi's wife who gave her heart to Krishna and sacrificed her body".

---

4. dhasamuganaich seRREnO pirATTiyaip pOlE

ச. தசமுகனைச் செற்றேனோ பிராட்டியைப் போலே

Ravana is called *dasa mugan* (one with ten heads) and Sita is known as *pirATTi*. The word *'seRRal'* either means to destroy or to look down upon. It is not appropriate to say the Sita destroyed Ravana or was even responsible for his destruction. Even though She could have killed him Herself, She did not do so. In fact, She tried Her best to make Ravana see reason and either surrender to or make friends with Sri Rama. She gave up Her ability to destroy Ravana or save Herself and waited for Rama to come and rescue Her.

What She did do was to look down upon Ravana, his wealth (something that would amaze even Hanuman) and the pleasures that he pointed out to Sita, to try and tempt Her. She treated them as dirt (note the incident when She placed a piece of grass between Herself and Ravana and addressed it when talking to him). She was willing to stay imprisoned (*'siRai irundhavaL'*) and suffer torture rather than agree to his advances.

She placed both Her body and soul as belonging to Rama and keeping Him in Her mind always, She simply waited for Him.

Thirukkolur Ammal asks "Can I be like Piratti and place everything completely in His hands".

Vaarththai 5

5. piNam ezhuppi viTTEnO thoNDaimAnaip pOlE

ரு. பிணம் எழுப்பி விட்டேனோ தொண்டைமானைப்
போலே

The king Thondaiman was an ardent devotee of Lord Srinivasa. It is to this king that Srinivasa had given His conch and discus, and had been without them for a long time.

One time a brahmin called Koorman decided to go to Kasi and give up his body in the Ganges. But he died in his hometown itself. His son called Krishna Sharma, decided to place his father's remains in the Ganges river. So, he brought his wife and children to King Thondaiman and placed them in his protection. Then he left for Kasi.

The king asked his workers to take care of Krishna Sharma's wife and children. Being involved in his daily duties, he completely forgot about them. The workers did not take good care of the family and they died.

After a while, Krishna Sharma came back and asked the king to return his family to him. That's when the king remembered about them. When he went to look for them, he found only their dead bodies. Shocked at this and not knowing what to do, he came back and told Krishna Sharma that his family had gone to Thirumalai and would be returning in a couple of days.

Between Srinivasa's sannidhi at Thirumalai and the king's palace, there was a secret passage. Taking that, the king went in front of the Lord and fell at His feet. He prayed for the Lord's grace and asked that either the Lord save him from this predicament or take him to His divine feet. The Lord who had deep affection for the king showered His divine grace on the king and told him to take some holy water from the sannidhi and sprinkle it on the dead bodies and make them come alive.

The king then returned to the palace and brought the family back to life. He returned the family to Krishna Sharma along with much wealth.

Thirukkolur Ammal is asking "Am I like the king who had great love for the Lord and was the recipient of His divine grace".

Vaarththai 6

6. piNa virundhiTTEnO kaNDAkarNanaip pOlE

சு. பிண விருந்திட்டேனோ கண்டாகர்ணனைப் போலே

Kandakarnan was a spirit that ate dead bodies. He was an ardent devotee of Shiva and as such hung a bell in his ear to prevent him from hearing Narayana's name. Hence he was called 'kaNdAkarNan'. One time he went to Kailasha and prayed to Shiva to help him leave the spirit state and attain moksha. Shiva told him that he could not give him liberation (moksha) and that only Narayana could do that. However, he gave the spirit a suggestion.

Shiva said "Lord Narayana has appeared on earth as Sri Krishna now. I asked Him one time to give me an opportunity to give Him a boon. He agreed and told me that He would come to Kailasha as Krishna and get a boon from me. When He comes here for that, if you pray to Him, He will give you what you seek".

He also gave a description of Krishna's form to Kandakarna so he would recognize Krishna when he saw Him. Kandakarna then thanked Shiva, removed the bell from his ear and keeping Krishna's image and name in his mind, started waiting for His arrival.

One day, he saw Krishna from a distance and recognized Him right away. Immediately he killed a rishi who was nearby, with a spear and brought the body to Krishna. Stopping Krishna he said "I have heard from Shiva that You are the one capable of giving moksha. I just now killed this rishi and brought his body just for You. Please accept my offering" and prayed to Him sincerely. He did that because the shastras say that, whatever a person eats according to his state, he should offer that to the divinity that he prays to, before eating it.

Since he had offered something to Krishna and only to Him, with great sincerity, Krishna accepted the offering and granted him moksha. He also granted moksha to Kandakarna's brother, based on his request. It is understood that the rishi who was killed by Kandakarna and offered to Krishna also attained moksha.

Thirukkolur Ammal is asking "Am I capable of praying to the Lord as sincerely as Kandakarna did".

Vaarththai 7

7. thAyk kOlam seydhEnO anasUyaip pOlE

எ. தாய்க் கோலம் செய்தேனோ அநசூயைப் போலே

After Sri Rama went to the forest based on His father's boons to Kaikeyi, He spent some time at Chithrakoodam along with Sita and Lakshmana. It was here that Bharatha tried to get Him to go back to Ayodhya. Fearing further requests from the people in Ayodhya, Rama left Chithrakoodam.

He then reached the sage Athri's ashrama and prayed to him as well as his wife Anasuya. Athri Maharishi introduced his wife to Sita and said "Anasuya is a great pativrata. She follows the path of dharma. One time when there was a famine here, she created vegetables and tubers and also made the Ganges flow. Pray to her like she is Your mother". Rama too said the same and Sita prayed to Anasuya and asked about her well being.

Anasuya was pleased by this and told Sita "I appreciate You leaving all the palace pleasures and following Your husband to the forest. A true wife is one who follows her husband even during his tough times. May You gain all good things".

Considering Sita as her own daughter, Anasuya then decorated Her with flowers and garments, and listened to Her full story. In the evening she told Sita "O Lady of sweet words! I am pleased by Your words. It is getting dark and You should go back to Your husband".

Sita bowed to her as She would to Her mother and went to Rama. Rama was also pleased by the affection shown by Anasuya to Sita. Rama and Sita then spent the night in that ashrama.

Thirukkolur Ammal is asking "Can I show the motherly affection to Thayar (the divine consort) that Anasuya showed".

Vaarththai 8

8. thandhai engE enREnO dhuruvanaip pOlE

அ. தந்தை எங்கே என்றேனோ துருவனைப் போலே

Svayambhuvamanu was born out of Brahma's body, He married Satharupai and had two sons called Priyamaratha and Uththanapadha. Uththanapadha became king and married two women called Suneethi and Suruchi. Through them both, he had two sons - Suneethi's son was called Dhruva and Suruchi's son was called Uththama.

Uththanapadha was very fond of Suruchi and ignored Suneethi altogether. When Dhruva was five years old, he asked his mother to go see his father. Suneethi told him about the king's palace and Dhruva went there to see him. Uththanapadha ignored Dhruva and in his presence took Uththama in his lap and was affectionate to him. When Dhruva tried to approach his father, Suruchi prevented him from doing so and used harsh words to chase him away.

Feeling both sad and angry, Dhruva went back to his mother and told her what happened. Suneethi then consoled him and told him "Pray to the father of everyone, Vasudeva (Sriman Narayana). If you do that and follow the path of Dharma, you will live a great life".

Dhruva left for the forest to pray to Vasudeva. In the forest, he obtained the Vasudeva mantra (Dvadasakshari) from the Saptharishis (or from Narada) and started meditating on Vasudeva. He kept the mantra in his mind and performed deep penance for a long time.

Pleased with him, Sriman Narayana appeared before him. He gave Dhruva divine knowledge and also a place amongst the stars (the pole star).

Thirukkolur Ammal is asking "Do I have the deep faith that Dhruva had and the great devotion he showed to the father of the Universe".

Vaarththai 9

9. mUnRezhuththuch sonnEnO kShathrabandhuvaip pOlE

கூ.   மூன்றெழுத்துச்   சொன்னேனோ   கூத்ரபந்துவைப்
போலே

Kshathrabandhu was the son of King Vishvaratha. His real name is not known. Kshathrabandhu means the lowest person amongst Kshatriyas. Because of his lowly character, he got this name. Unable to tolerate his behavior, the people of the kingdom chased him into the forest. However, even in the forest he continued his ways of torturing others.

One time, a rishi came into the forest where he was staying. Due to the extreme heat, the rishi became very thirsty. Seeing a pond he went there to drink the water, slipped and fell into the pond. When Kshathrabandhu saw this, somehow he felt pity for the rishi and pulled him out of the pond. Then he gave him something to eat and massaged his body.

The rishi woke up and asked Kshathrabandhu his story and why he was living in such a forest. Kshathrabandhu told him his entire history without hiding anything. Wishing to correct him, the rishi gave him some good advise.

Kshathrabandhu replied "O Rishi! My bad nature was born with me and will not leave me. There is no point trying to make me a better person".

The rishi then taught him the Lord's divine name Govinda which is made of three aksharas. He then told Kshathrabandhu to keep repeating this nAma even if he continues in his bad ways.

From that day onward, Kshathrabandhu started repeating the Lord's name all the time. Because of that, after his death, he was reborn as a Brahmin and became an ardent devotee of the Lord. After that, he attained the Lord's feet.

His story has been sung by Thondaradippodi Azhvar in his divya prabandham called Thirumaalai.

Thirukkolur Ammal is asking "Did I spend my time saying the Lord's name made up of three aksharas, like Kshathrabandhu did".

Vaarththai 10

10. mudhalaDiyaip peRREnO agaligaiyaip pOlE

க0. முதலடியைப் பெற்றேனோ அகலிகையைப் போலே

'*mudhaladi*' refers to the Lord's divine feet.

Gauthama maharishi's wife was named Ahalya. Hearing about her great beauty, Indra became enamored with her. When Gauthama maharishi went to the river to take a bath, he took the rishi's form and approached Ahalya and she allowed herself to be duped by him.

Before Indra could leave, Gauthama rishi came back and saw Indra. He cursed him that he would lose his masculinity. He also cursed Ahalya saying "You will become an atom within the ashes in the ashrama (some stories state that she was cursed to be a stone) and perform penance for a thousand years. At that time Sriman Narayana will be born as Sri Rama and will be brought here by Vishvamitra. You will be released by the touch of His divine feet and then can join me". Gauthama rishi then left the place.

After a thousand years, Vishvamitra rishi took Rama to his place for the protection of his yaga. After the completion of the yaga, he took Rama to Mithila. On the way, he brought Him to Gauthama's ashrama. By the touch of His feet, Ahalya's curse was removed and she became pure. Gauthama rishi also came back there at that time and accepted her.

Thirukkolur Ammal is asking "Did I have the great fortune of gaining the touch of the Lord's divine feet like Ahalya did".

Vaarththai 11

11. pinjchAyp pazhuththEnO ANDALaip pOlE

க க. பிஞ்சாய்ப் பழுத்தேனோ ஆண்டாளைப் போலே

Andal is the incarnation of Bhu Devi and was found in the garden of Periyazhvar under a Tulsi plant. Periyazhvar brought her up as his own daughter. Not surprisingly, Periyazhvar's love for Sri Krishna also manifested in Andal, and She developed great love for Him even at a tender age (it is said that She wrote Thiruppavai at the age of five). This love came out as two great works which are part of the 4000 Divya Prabandhams – Thiruppavai and Nachchiyar Thirumozhi. Through both, She declared Her surrender to the Lord and that She would not belong to any other.

In his Upadesa Raththinamalai, Manavala Mamunigal states:

anjchu kuDikkoru sandhadhiyAy AzhvArgal
tham seyalai vinjchi niRkum thanmaiyaLAy - pinjchAyp
pazhuththALai ANDALai nALum paththhiyuDan
vazhuththhAy manamE magizhndhu

Thirukkolur Ammal is asking "Did I show great love for Sri Krishna at a tender age like Andal did".

Vaarththai 12

12. emperumAn enREnO paTTar pirAnaip pOlE

க உ. எம்பெருமான் என்றேனோ பட்டர் பிரானைப்
போலே

Pattar Piran is the name for Periyazhvar. Periyazhvar lived in Srivilliputtur where he maintained a flower garden and made garlands for Lord Vatapatrasayee every day.

The king of that area, Vallabha Deva arranged for a debate to determine the true Supreme Lord and announced that the winner would get a prize of gold coins ('*kizhi*'). The Lord appeared in Periyazhvar's dream and told him to go to the king's court and make the determination that He is the supreme and win the prize. Accepting His word as command, Periyazhvar, who had no formal education from a teacher, went to the court and proved with all pramANas that Sriman Narayana is the supreme being. Pleased by that, the king placed him on his own elephant and took him around the city with praises. Sriman Narayana then appeared on Garuda with His consorts to see Periyazhvar. It is then that Periyazhvar sang the magnificent Thiruppallandu pasuram.

In that pasuram, he sang *'ennAL emperumAn! undhanukku aDiyOm enRu ezhuththuppaTTa annALE'*. Through that he showed His absolute supremacy and his natural servitude.

Thirukkolur Ammal is asking "Did I learn my true nature and call out to Him as my Lord like Periyazhvar did".

Vaarththai 13

13. ArAyndhu viTTEnO thirumazhisaiyAr pOlE

க ந. ஆராய்ந்து விட்டேனோ திருமழிசையார் போலே

Thirumazhisai Azhvar was born to Bhargava maharishi and Kanakangi, a divine damsel, in the kshetram of Thirumazhisai. He was abandoned by his mother as soon as we was born and was picked up by a low caste person who brought him up as his own son. Due to the grace of Lord Jagannatha of Thirumazhisai and being the son of a great rishi, he grew up with great knowledge of the shastras.

He began to join and analyze various sampradhayams and eventually settled on Shaivism. At that time, Peyazhvar met him and through debate won him back into the Srivaishnava sampradhayam. He gained fame as a great devotee of the Lord and after much traveling settled in the divyadesam of Thirukkudandhai, from where he attained the Lord's divine feet.

He describes his journey into various religions and eventually reaching Srivaishnavam in his own words:

*sAkkiyam kaRROm samaN kaRROm sankaranAr
Akkkiya Agama nUl ArAyndhOm - bAkkiyaththAl*

sengkaTkariyAnaich sErndhOm yAm thIdhilamE
engkaTkariyadhonRil

Thirukkolur Ammal is asking "Did I analyze other religions and gave them up as false like Thirumazhisaip Piran did".

Vaarththai 14

14. nAn (avan) siRiyan enREnO AzhvAraip pOlE

க ச. நான் (அவன்) சிறியன் என்றேனோ ஆழ்வாரைப்
போலே

The word Azhvar refers to Swami Nammazhvar. In spite of being given the flawless knowledge (*'mayaRvaRa madhinalam'*) by Sriman Narayana Himself, in many of his pasurams he expresses his lowliness (*naichyanusandhanam*) to Him. In Thiruvaymozhi 3-3-4, he says *'nIsanEn niRai onRumilEn'*. In Thiruvaymozhi 4-7-1, he says *'sIlamillAch siRiyan'*.

Thirukkolur Ammal is asking "Did I understand my true nature and practice naichyanusandhanam like Azhvar did".

In Periya Thiruvandhadhi 75, Azhvar says:

puviyum iruvisumbum nin agaththa nI en
seviyin vazhi pugundhu ennuLLAy - avivinRi
yAn periyan nI periyai enbadhanai yAr aRivAr?
Un parugu nEmiyAy! uLLu

In this pasuram, he shows the Lord to be the owner of everything - this world and paramapadham. He then expresses his amazement that this Lord is inside him. Being that, he asks the question, 'Who knows if You are big or if I am big'. This is also broken a little differently. It could also be said that Azhvar is saying *'yAn periyan'*; *'nI periyai enbadhanai yAr aRivAr?'* – that is, 'I am big, who knows if you are big?'.

This is *sAtvika ahankAram* of Azhvar. He is amazed that One who swallowed everything has allowed Himself to be inside Azhvar for ever. This only goes to show His greatness.

Because of this pasuram, Azhvar is called by the name *'periyan'* in Azhvar Thirunagari. It is also said that this pasuram is the reason why this work is called Periya Thiruvandhadhi, even though it is made of only 87 pasurams, unlike other Andhadhis in the 4000 divya prabandham which have 100 or more verses.

Thirukkolur Ammal may also be asking "Am I capable of speaking like Azhvar did".

Vaarththai 15

15. EdhEnum enREnO kulasEkarar pOlE

க டு. ஏதேனும் என்றேனோ குலசேகரர் போலே

Kulasekhara Azhvar's pasurams are called Perumal Thirumozhi. In this work, he has sung a padhigam on Thiruvengadamudaiyan – *'UnERu selvaththu'*. In these pasurams, he expresses his desire to be born in any fashion on the divine mountain of Thirumalai. He asks that he be born as a bird, a fish, a tree, a path, a river, etc on the mountain. He also prays that he be born as the doorstep to the temple of the Lord. This is why the inner doorstep of divyadesam temples are called 'Kulasekaran Padi'. He finally asks that he be born as anything on Thirumalai – *'emperumAn ponmalai mEl EdhEnum AvEnE'*.

In this relation, Anandazhvan mentioned the following: "EdhEnum means Azhvar is ready to even lose his true nature of being subservient to the Lord and become the Lord Himself, if it means that he could be on Thirumalai hills".

Bhattar said "EdhEnum means, let Azhvar not know who or what he is, let even the Lord not know who or what he is, let no one know or praise him. Just let him be something on Thirumalai".

Thirukkolur Ammal is asking "Did I wish to be always on Thirumalai like Kulasekhara Azhvar did".

---

16. yAn sathyam enREnO krushNanaip pOlE

க சூ. யான் ஸத்யம் என்றேனோ க்ருஷ்ணனைப் போலே

It is said by our Purvacharyas that the truth spoken by Sri Rama and the falsehoods uttered by Sri Krishna are our refuge. However, in this statement by Thirukkolur Ammal it is shown that Sri Krishna too spoke only the truth.

Just as Rama was described as *'rAmo vigrahavAn dharma'* so too Krishna is described as *'sanAtana dharma'*. On his deathbed, Bheeshma pointed out to Yudishtra that Krishna is dharma personified.

Krishna's words uttered for the protection of His devotees, may appear like falsehoods, but they are not.

When He went as the messenger for the Pandavas, Draupadi asked that He help her take her revenge on the Kauravas. At that time, Krishna stated that "The sky might fall down; the Earth may crumble; the Himalayas may break down into pieces; the oceans may become dry; even if all these improbable things were to come true, my words will never be falsified".

Sanjaya too calls Krishna as truth personified.

When Uththarai's son was born lifeless like charred wood due to Ashvaththama's arrow, a voice was heard stating that, if one who is a true brahmachari and a speaker of nothing but truth was to touch the baby, he would gain life. When no one stepped forward, Krishna did. And with the touch of His divine lotus feet, the child came alive.

His words are always true. This is what is being established by Thirukkolur Ammal.

Vaarththai 17

17. aDaiyALam sonnEnO kabandhanaip pOlE
க எ. அடையாளம் சொன்னேனோ கபந்தனைப் போலே

In the vamsa of Dhanu was born Kabandha as the son of the king Sri. He was disrespectful to a rishi called Stulasiras and was cursed by him to have a very large body. Later he performed a severe penance toward Brahma and was blessed with a long life. He then went to war with Indra. Indra hit him with his Vajrayuda and pushed his thighs into his stomach and his head into his chest. Because he was blessed by Brahma with a long life, Indra could not kill him. Instead he gave Kabandha two long arms, a mouth with large canine teeth in his stomach and a single burning red eye. Indra also told him that when Sri Rama and Lakshmana cut his arms off, his curse would be lifted. Kabandha then lived in the Krauncharanya forest. He stayed in one place and would catch anything that got within his arms reach and eat it.

After Ravana abducted Sita, Rama and Lakshmana came through Krauncharanya in search of Her. Kabandha caught them with his long hands and tried to eat them. When they cut off his hands, he realized that they were Rama and Lakshmana and asked that they burn his body. When they did that, he regained his original form.

He then told them the following: "Sugreeva who is the son of Surya, is currently living in the Rishyamukha mountain, after having been chased away by his brother Vali. He is one with good qualities and will help You in Your search for Sita. Accept his friendship and through his help You will gain back Sita." He then told Rama and Lakshmana how to meet Sugreeva and then went to heaven.

Thirukkolur Ammal is asking "Did I give any help to the Lord like Kabandha did".

Vaarththai 18

18. andharangkam sonnEnO thrijaDaiyaip pOlE

க அ. அந்தரங்கம் சொன்னேனோ த்ரிஜடையைப் போலே

Trijada was a servant of Ravana and one of the rakshasis that he had ordered to guard Sita in the Ashoka Vanam.

After Sita was kept under guard by Ravana for many months, not seeing Sri Rama coming to rescue Her, She became broken hearted. She was unable to handle the harsh words and demands of the rakshasis around Her. Seeing that, Trijada told the rakshasis of a dream that she had and chased them away. In that dream, she said, "I saw Ravana wearing a red dress and heading south while seated on a donkey. I also saw Rama wearing a white dress with white flowers, looking like Vishnu, fly in from the sky in a golden palanquin and carry Sita around on an elephant. Therefore, Rama will definitely defeat Ravana and take Sita away. If you wish to survive, it is better to surrender to Sita and beg Her pardon".

Later, during the war between Rama and Ravana, she brought news of the many victories of Rama's army to Sita.

When Indrajit made Rama and Lakshmana faint with his nagastra, the rakshasas took Sita to the battlefield and claimed that they both were dead. When Sita shed tears due to great sadness, Trijada consoled Her by saying "Do not fear. Rama and Lakshmana have only fainted. They cannot be killed by the arrows of these rakshasas".

Thus, Trijada helped Piratti in many ways.

Thirukkolur Ammal is asking "Am I capable of giving the kind of help Trijada did by being a confidante and giving timely advice".

Vaarththai 19

19. avan dheyvam enREnO maNDOdhariyaip pOlE
கூ. அவன் தெய்வம் என்றேனோ மண்டோதரியைப்
போலே

Mandodhari was the wife and queen of Ravana. She was the daughter of Maya, the architect of the devas. She was also a great pativrata. When Ravana captured Sita and brought Her to Lanka, she advised Ravana that it was a great mistake to kidnap Her and that it would lead to great destruction. She also advised him to seek Rama's friendship.

Ravana did not listen to her and eventually went into war with Rama and Lakshmana. At the end, he was defeated and killed by Rama. His many wives then came to the battlefield and cried over his dead body. At that time, Mandodhari said the following: "Rama is not just an ordinary human being. Sriman Narayana, who carries the divine weapons of Shanka and Chakra, killed you. You did not listen to the good advise I gave you. The improper desire that you had for the great pativrata Sita is what caused this end. There is no doubt that Sri Vishnu came down as Rama and killed you".

Thirukkolur Ammal is asking "Am I capable of understanding avatara rahasya and talking about it like Mandodhari did".

Vaarththai 20

20. aham vEdhmi enREnO visvAmithraraip pOlE

உ0. அஹம் வேத்மி என்றேனோ விஸ்வாமித்ரரைப்
போலே

One time the sage Vishvamitra came to king Dasaratha's court. The king received him with great honor and promised to fulfill his desires. The sage then asked Dasaratha to give him Sri Rama so that He can defend the sage's yaga from the rakshasas who were disturbing it. The king replied that Rama was very young and would not be able to accomplish that task and that he could come himself instead.

Vishvamitra replied: "O King! I know Sri Rama. He is capable of defeating the rakshasas. Only those who do penance like myself and Vasishta truly know who He is. Understand that my words are nothing but the truth."

aham vedmi mahAtmAnam rAmam satya parAkramam vasishTopi mahAtejA ye cheme tapasistithA:

Vasishta agreed with Vishvamitra and asked the king to send Rama and Lakshmana along with him. The king agreed and the two princes went with the sage and helped protect his yaga against the likes of Tataka and Maricha.

Thirukkolur Ammal is asking "Am I capable of understanding the truth and speaking it like Vishvamitra did".

Vaarththai 21

21. dhEvu maRRaRiyEn enREnO madhurakaviyaip pOlE

உ.க. தேவு மற்றறியேன் என்றேனோ மதுரகவியைப்
போலே

Madhurakavi Azhvar was born in the divyadesam of Thirukkolur near Azhvar Thirunagari. He was on a yatra to the North when he saw a divine light in the southern sky. Following it, he reached Azhvar Thirunagari and found Swami Nammazhvar. He then tested him and realizing the greatness of Azhvar fell at his feet and became his disciple.

He then considered his acharya Nammazhvar as everything - mother, father, acharya and God - to him ('*annaiyAy aththanAy*'). He expressed that in his divine work Kanninun Siruththambu - a work dedicated entirely to Nammazhvar.

In that work, occurs the following pasuram:

nAvinAl naviRRu inbam eydhinEn
mEvinEn avan ponnadi meymmaiyE
dhEvu maRRaRiyEn kurugUr nambi
pAvin innisai pAdith thirivanE

In this pasuram, Madhurakavi Azhvar states that he knows no God other than Nammazhvar (*'dhEvu maRRu aRiyEn'*). He not only is renouncing the things of this world, but he is rejecting the other world and even Him, in favor of his acharya. This is the status of Sri Shathrugna who ignored even Sri Rama and was devoted only to Sri Bharatha.

The philosophy of following one's acharya as everything, demonstrated by Srivaishnava Acharyas (*'AchArya abhimAnamE uththAragam'*) arose from Madhurakavi Azhvar's Acharya bhakti.

Thirukkolur Ammal is asking "Did I demonstrate Acharya bhakti like Madhurakavi Azhvar did".

---

22. dheyvaththaip peRREnO dhEvakiyAr pOlE

உ உ. தெய்வத்தைப் பெற்றேனோ தேவகியார் போலே

During the time Brahma's son Svayambhuvamanu ruled this earth, Sutapas and his wife Pruchni prayed to Narayana for a long time. When He appeared before them and asked what they wanted, they asked for a son like Him to be born to them. He blessed them and He Himself was born to them as Pruchnigarba. When they were reborn as Kashyapa and Atiti, He came as their son Vamana. They were reborn for a third time as Vasudeva and Devaki.

In that birth, Devaki was born as the younger sister of Kamsa. After their wedding, a divine voice was heard announcing that their eighth son would kill Kamsa. So, Kamsa put them both in jail and began to kill their children one by one as they were born. The eighth child was born inside the jail in the month of Avani in the star Rohini in Ashtami thithi, at midnight. That child was Krishna who told them how He was born to them three times.

Thirukkolur Ammal is asking "Did I do severe penance and give birth to the Lord Himself like Devaki did".

Vaarththai 23

23. Azhi maRai enREnO vasudhEvaraip pOlE

உ ங. ஆழி மறை என்றேனோ வசுதேவரைப் போலே

When Sri Krishna was born to Devaki and Vasudeva, He came bearing His weapons such as Shanka and Chakra (*'devakI pUrvasandhyAm AvirbhUtam mahAtmanA'*). Devaki and Vasudeva prayed to Him to hide His form as they were worried that Kamsa would cause some harm to Him - this is the nature of doing mangaLAshAsanam to Him, without thinking about His stature and ours. This concern has been demonstrated by others such as the people of Ayodhya and Periyazhvar.

Krishna hid His form and changed into a normal human child. He then told them to carry Him to Gokulam and leave Him at Nandagopa and Yashoda's place. There He grew up and performed His avatara activities.

Thirukkolur Ammal is asking "Did I show great concern for Him like Devaki and Vasudeva did".

Vaarththai 24

24. Ayanai vaLarththEnO yasOdhaiyAraip pOlE

உ ச. ஆயனை வளர்த்தேனோ யசோதையாரைப் போலே

After Sri Krishna was born to Devaki and Vasudeva, He told them to take Him across the Yamuna river to Gokulam and leave Him there at Yashoda and Nandagopa's place. Vasudeva followed those instructions. Krishna then grew up as the son of Yashoda and she did not know any different.

Even though He was born in a kshatriya clan, He grew up as a cowherd yadava (Ayan) in their house. There were many instances in the childhood of Krishna where He showed his
Paratva, such as the time He showed all the worlds in His mouth to Yashoda. However, she continued to treat Him as her son only - by sending Him to herd the cows, teaching him to play the flute, tying Him up with a rope when He was mischievous, etc.

When He lifted the Govardhana mountain to protect the yadavas from the anger of Indra, they asked Him if He was a deva. He told them that He was their relative and that they should never separate themselves from Him.

Thirukkolur Ammal is asking "Did I bring up Krishna like Yashoda did (as one of her own)".

---

25. anuyAththiram seydhEnO aNilangaLaip pOlE

உ ரு. அநுயாத்திரம் செய்தேனோ அணிலங்களைப் போலே

After Sri Rama and Lakshmana assembled the army of monkeys along with the vAnara king Sugreeva, they marched toward Lanka in search of the abducted Sita and reached the ocean. To cross the ocean they decided to build a bridge across it. The monkey army got busy in this activity using rocks and boulders. At that time, the squirrels in the nearby forest also decided to help Rama's endeavor.

They jumped into the ocean and made their bodies wet, came back to the beach, rolled in the sand, went to the bridge and shook the sand from their bodies filling the gaps between the rocks. Their thought was to help drain the ocean by making their bodies wet and help build the bridge by adding sand to it.

Thondaradippodi Azhvar celebrated their service to the Lord in his Thirumaalai pasuram:

kurangkugaL malaiyai nUkkak kuLiththuth thAm puraNdiTTODi
tharanga nIr aDaikkaluRRa salamilA anilum pOlEn

Thirukkolur Ammal is asking "Did I do divine service by going behind the monkeys (anu yAtra) like the squirrels did".

Vaarththai 26

26. aval poriyai IndhEnO kuchElaraip pOlE

உ சூ. அவல் பொரியை ஈந்தேனோ குசேலரைப் போலே

Sri Krishna learned all the arts from the rishi Santhipini. His fellow student at that time was Sudama who was also known as Kuchela. Kuchela was a very poor brahmin. He had great knowledge and knew the truth about Krishna. As such he had great love for Him.

After the end of their studies, Kuchela went back home and married Suseelai and lived with her. He continued to be poor and survived on alms.

One time Suseelai approached Kuchela and told him "Your childhood friend Krishna is now king and ruling Dwaraka. Go see Him. He will help us get rid of our poverty".

Kuchela did not want to ask Krishna for anything, but he agreed to go, because it would be an opportunity to meet Him again. However, he did not want to go empty handed.

So, Suseelai borrowed some *aval* (fluffed rice) from her friends and gave it to Kuchela. With this small offering, Kuchela left to see Krishna.

Krishna received him with great honor and happiness at His palace. He sat him in His own seat and had Rukmini fan him. He then talked about the old days with Kuchela. Then, He asked Kuchela what he had brought for Him to eat. Kuchela was ashamed to give Him the small amount of *aval* that he had brought. Krishna would not leave him though and forced him to give the *aval* to Him. With great pleasure and claiming that it was more dear to Him than the butter in Gokulam, He ate a handful of the aval. As soon as He did that, His full grace had fallen on Kuchela. It is said that Rukmini stopped Him from eating any more of the *aval*.

Kuchela spent the night at the palace and left the next day without asking Krishna for anything. However, on his return, he found that his hut had become a great house and that his family had received great wealth. He continued to live a simple life while praising His greatness.

Thirukkolur Ammal is asking "Did I take aval with great affection to the Lord like Kuchela did".

Vaarththai 27

27. AyudhangkaL IndhEnO agasthiyaraip pOlE

உ எ. ஆயுதங்கள் ஈந்தேனோ அகஸ்தியரைப் போலே

When Sri Rama entered the Dandakaranya forest, He went to the ashramas of several maharishis and paid His respects to them. One of these rishis was the sage Agastya (who
is credited with being the one who put together the Tamil language).

Agastya received Rama with honor. Knowing Rama's avatara rahasya and what was to come, he presented Him with several weapons. He told Rama "See this bow which belongs to Vishnu. It was made by Vishvakarma. Using this bow, Mahavishnu killed many asuras and helped the devas. These two quivers which never reduce in arrows and this sword were given to me by Indra. Take these weapons." and gave his mangalashasanas to Him.

Thirukkolur Ammal is asking "Did I help the Lord like Agastya did".

Vaarththai 28

28. andharangkam pukkEnO sanjchayanaip pOlE

உ.அ. அந்தரங்கம் புக்கேனோ சஞ்சயனைப் போலே

Sanjaya was the charioteer for Dritharashtra and was also his close friend. They both learnt from the same guru in their young age. When the Kuaravas and Pandavas went to war in Kurukshetra, he acted as the eyes for the blind king and kept him up to date on the daily events in the war.

He told the king that whichever side Krishna and Arjuna were on, that would be the side that would emerge victorious:

yatra yogeshvara: krushNo yatra pArtho danurdhara:
tatra shrIrvijayobhUti: druvanIdirmatirmama

Before the war, Dritharashtra sent Sanjaya as his messenger to see Krishna. At that time, Krishna, His wife Satyabama, Arjuna and Draupadi were together in their private chambers having a discussion. No one was allowed in. When they heard of Sanjaya's visit, Krishna said "Let's have him meet us here. Seeing how close we are, he will take that message back to the Kauravas.

That itself will destroy them." And Sanjaya did take that message back to Duryodhana.

Thirukkolur Ammal is asking "Did I get a private audience with Him like Sanjaya did".

Vaarththai 29

29. karmaththAl peRREnO janakaraip pOlE

உ கூ. கர்மத்தால் பெற்றேனோ ஜனகரைப் போலே

King Janaka, despite being the ruler of a kingdom, was a great karma yogi. He carried on the rules of the shastras with detachment, control of his senses, without ahankara and mamakara, and without expecting anything in return. That is, he performed all his duties as per the shastras, as a service to the Lord.

One time his teacher Yagyavalka wanted to show his greatness to his other disciples. When all of them were at his ashrama, with his yogic power he made it appear that the kingdom of Mithila was completely on fire. When all the other disciples ran helter and skelter trying to save their meager belongings, King Janaka sat without moving, being in the state that nothing truly belonged to him.

In Bhagavad Gita, when Sri Krishna explains the karma yoga, He says *'karmaNyaivahi samsiddhim AsthitA janakAtaya:'* - saying that rAjarishis such as Janaka attained siddhi through karma yoga.

Thirukkolur Ammal is asking "Am I capable of being steady in karma yoga like Janaka".

Vaarththai 30

30. kaDiththu avanaik kaNDEnO thirumangkaiyAr pOlE

௩0. கடித்து அவனைக் கண்டேனோ திருமங்கையார்
போலே

Thirumangai Azhvar wanted to marry the beautiful Kumudavalli Nachchiyar. She demanded that he prove his worth by feeding the devotees of Sriman Narayana every day. He agreed and spent all his wealth on that. After running out of funds, wishing to continue the service, he became a highway thief and used the stolen money for this purpose.

In order to shower their grace on Azhvar, the Lord and His divine consort dressed themselves as a newly-wed young couple and wearing many ornaments appeared in front of him at a place called Thirumanangkollai. Azhvar stopped them with a sword in hand and demanded all their jewelry. When it came to a ring worn on the feet of the Lord, he was unable to take it off. So, Azhvar used his teeth to bite the ring and take it off His feet.

Then he put them all together into a sack and tried to pick it up, but it was too heavy for him. So, he demanded the Lord to tell him what mantra He had used to make it that heavy (Azhvar was wondering if such a slender young lad could carry these jewels on Him, why the strong Azhvar was unable to lift them). When he threatened the Lord with a sword, He spoke the great Thirumantra in Azhvar's ears.

That opened Azhvar's inner eyes and he truly saw the Lord. He became Thirumangai Azhvar in that moment and began singing the magnificent *'vAdinEn'* pasuram.

Thirukkolur Ammal is asking "Did I get the opportunity to attain His grace by biting Him like Thirumangai Azhvar did".

Vaarththai 31

31. kuDai mudhalAnadhu AnEnO ananthAzhvAn pOlE

ந க. குடை முதலானது ஆனேனோ அனந்தாழ்வான் போலே

AnanthazhvAn is the name for Adisesha on whom the Lord rests. He is always with the Lord. Even when He descends to this world, Adisesha accompanies Him in some form and performs services to Him. Since he is in eternal service and is the personification of service, he is called Adisesha.

Poygai Azhvar sings in his Mudhal Thiruvandhadhi about him thus:

senRAL kuDaiyAm irundhAl singAsanamAm
ninRAl maravaDiyAm nILkaDaluL enRum
puNaiyAm maNi viLakkAm pUmpaTTAm pulgum
aNaiyAm thirumARku aravu

Alavandar too describes him in a similar fashion in his Stotra Ratnam.

Azhvar says Thiruvananthazhvan is an umbrella when He walks, he is a seat when He sits, he is the footwear when He stands up, he is the float when He is in the milky ocean, he is a lamp, he is a cloth and he is a pillow. Thus, he is everything when it comes to rendering service.

Thirukkolur Ammal is asking "Have I rendered any kind of service to Him like Adisesha does in various forms".

Vaarththai 32

32. koNDu thirindhEnO thiruvaDiyaip pOlE

௩உ. கொண்டு திரிந்தேனோ திருவடியைப் போலே

The term thiruvaDi refers to both Garuda (*periya thiruvaDi*) and Hanuman (*siRiya thiruvaDi*). They got these names because they both perform the service of carrying the Lord. Just as Adisesha does various services (see previous Vaarththai), so too Garuda acts as the Lord's friend, His servant, His conveyance, His seat, His flag, His umbrella, and so on. Azhvars refer many times to the fact that the Lord rides Garuda and performs various acts.

During His avatara as Sri Rama, Hanuman carried Him and Lakshmana on a few occasions. When they first arrive to meet Sugreeva, He talks to them and then carries them on his shoulders to Sugreeva. Later when Rama and Lakshmana wage a war against Ravana, he carries them again on his shoulders so that they do not have to stand on the ground and fight.

Thirukkolur Ammal is asking "Did I carry the Lord on my shoulders with affection, like Hanuman did".

Vaarththai 33

33. iLaippu viDAy thIrththEnO nampADuvAn pOlE

ந ந. இளைப்பு விடாய் தீர்த்தேனோ நம்பாடுவான்
போலே

In Sri Varaha Purana, Varaha Perumal tells Bhudevi the greatness of singing His praise and the benefits that it gives the devotee. This section is known as Kaisika Mahatmyam and within it is the story of the devotee Nampaduvan who sang the Lord's praises all the time.

In south India near the Ksheera river was Siddhashrama. Here, a low caste person would come every day early in the morning from a long distance and sing the Lord's praises. He did this for several years. Sri Varaha called him *'mama gAyaka'* and therefore his name became Nampaduvan.

One time, in the month of Karththikai on sukla paksha Dwadasi, he stayed awake in the night and left very early to go sing about the Lord. On the way, a brahmarakshas caught him and wanted to eat him. Nampaduvan requested the brahmarakshas to let him go so he can go and sing to Perumal. He promised that he would return and allow himself to be eaten. The brahmarakshas did not trust him and Nampaduvan started saying that he would attain a certain sin if he did not return. Only when he swore that he would get the sin of equating Sriman Narayana with other devatas if he did not return, did the brahmarakshas let him go.

Namapduvan went to Thirukkurungudi divyadesam, sang about the Lord and returned as promised. The brahmarakshas was a brahmin called Somasharma in his previous birth. Because he committed a sin during a yaga, he was born as a brahmarakshas. Determining that he would be liberated only by Nampaduvan, he asked for the fruit of Nampaduvan's singing that night so that he may let him go alive. Nampaduvan did not agree. After some more requests, Nampaduvan finally agreed to give him the fruit of his singing one song sung in the Kaisika meter. Receiving that, the brahmarakshas was liberated, was reborn in a good family and finally attained moksha.

Thirukkolur Ammal is asking "Did I sing and liberate someone from their birth as a rakshasa, like Nampaduvan did".

Vaarththai 34

34. iDaikazhiyil kaNDEnO mudhalAzhvArgaLaip pOlE

ந ச. இடைகழியில் கண்டேனோ முதலாழ்வார்களைப்
போலே

Mudhal Azhvargal are the first three Azhvars to appear in this world. They are Poygai Azhvar, Bhoothaththazhvar and Peyazhvar. They were born in three different flowers in the divyadesams of Kanchi, Mallai and Mayilai. Having been given the flawless knowledge by the Lord they went from one place to another every day and experienced Him.

The Lord decided to bring them all together in the divyadesam of Thirukkovalur. On a dark and stormy night, Poygaiyazhvar arrived first and sought shelter in the ashrama of Mrugandu Maharishi. He was resting in the *iDai kazhi* (the area between the front and back of the house). Soon after, Bhoothaththazhvar arrived to the same place. They both were able to sit comfortably. Then came Peyazhvar and the three were able to only stand in the narrow area. Shortly after that, the three Azhvars realized that a fourth person was amongst them and pushing against all of them.

Realizing it was the Lord Himself, Poygaiyazhvar lit a lamp through a verse – *'vaiyam thagaLiyA vArkadalE neyyAga veyya kadhirOn viLAkkAga'*. This became the first verse of Mudhal Thiruvandhadhi. In this verse,

Azhvar made this world the cup, the ocean as the ghee and the Sun as the light.

Bhoothaththazhvar lit another lamp through a verse – *'anbE thagaLiyA ArvamE neyyAga inburugu sindhai iduthiriyA'*. This became the first verse of Irandam Thiruvandhadhi. In this verse, Azhvar made his love as the cup, his passion as the ghee and his thought as the lamp.

In the light of the two lamps, Peyazhvar saw the Lord with His divine consort and sang the verse *'thirukkaNdEn pon mEni kaNdEn'*. This became the first verse of Moondram Thiruvandhadhi.

All three Azhvars thus saw the Lord in the narrow area of the ashrama and sang the first pasurams of the Nalayira Divyaprabandham.

Thirukkolur Ammal is asking "Did I receive the grace of the Lord to see Him, like the first three Azhvars did".

Vaarththai 35

35. iru mannar peRREnO vAlmIkiyaip pOlE

நடரு. இரு மன்னர் பெற்றேனோ வால்மீகியைப் போலே

After the coronation at Ayodhya, Sri Rama ruled the kingdom for a long time. At one time, when Sita had become pregnant, Rama heard that a washerman spoke ill of the fact that He had brought back Sita who was imprisoned in Ravana's place and made Her His queen.

During this time, Sita had asked a boon from Rama that She be allowed to live in the forest for a while. So, Rama asked Lakshmana to take Her to the forest and leave Her near Valmiki Maharishi's ashrama. Lakshmana followed the order of Rama.

Valmiki Maharishi took Sita to his ashrama and protected Her there. After a while Sita gave birth to the twins Lava and Kucha. When they were born, Valmiki blessed them by rubbing one child with the tip of the darba grass and the other with its root - the tip of this grass is called Kucham and the root is called Lavam - thus the boys were named.

Valmiki acted as their guardian and brought them up as worthy sons of Rama. He taught them all vidyas and also the Ramayana story.

Thirukkolur Ammal is asking "Did I do service to the Lord and brought up the two princes, like Valmiki did".

Vaarththai 36

36. irumAlai IndhEnO thoNDaraDippoDiyAr pOlE

நீ சூ. இருமாலை ஈந்தேனோ தொண்டரடிப்பொடியார்
போலே

Thondaradippodi Azhvar lived in Srirangam and just like Periyazhvar at Srivilliputtur, he too maintained a garden and performed flower service to the Lord. He would make beautiful garlands and present them to Sri Ranganatha daily.

The word 'iru' in this Vaarththai of Thirukkolur Ammal has two meanings - one is great and the other is two.

If used in the first sense, then we can say that Azhvar provided great and wonderful flower garlands to the Lord. They were great because Azhvar considered himself as the dust under the feet of bhAgavatas - thoNdar adip podi - and gave the garlands only as pure service to the Lord. Also, Azhvar wrote amazing word garlands to the Lord through his works Thirumaalai and Thiruppaliyezhuchchi.

If used in the second sense - that is, two - then we can say Azhvar provided two wonderful garlands to the Lord. One was a 'pU mAlai' – that is, a flower garland and the other was a 'pA mAlai' - that is, a word garland.

We can also say that the number two refers to the two word garlands that Azhvar wrote - Thirumaalai and Thiruppalliyezhuchchi.

Thirukkolur Ammal is asking "Did I provide the Lord with such great garlands, as Thondaradippodi Azhvar did".

---

37. avan uraikkap peRREnO thirukkachchiyAr pOlE

ந எ. அவன் உரைக்கப் பெற்றேனோ திருக்கச்சியார்
போலே

Sri Kanchi Poorna (Thirukkachchi Nambigal)'s name was Gajendra Dasa. He was born in a family of merchants.

His father once gave him a large sum of money and asked him to invest and grow it. Nambigal spent it all in the service of the Lord and His devotees. After a couple of years, his father asked him about the money and where he had invested it. Nambigal said that he had invested it in the divine abode of the Lord. His father became angry with him and so Nambigal left his household and went to Srirangam, where he began to do service at the divine feet of his acharya Swami Alavandar. Later, per his acharya's order, he returned to Kanchi and started doing fan service to Sri Varadaraja Perumal. When the two were alone, Sri Varadaraja would sometimes talk to him.

Ramanuja who was known as Ilaiyazhvar at that time, was residing in Kanchi as well. He wanted to become Nambigal's disciple but Nambigal did not accept it stating that as a a Vaisya he could not accept Ilaiyazhvar who was a brahmin, as his disciple. Ramanuja then asked Nambigal if he could ask Varadaraja about the questions in his mind. Nambigal agreed and that night placed Ramanuja's request to the Lord.

Varadaraja gave six answers to Nambigal and told him that those would answer the questions in Ramanuja's mind. The six replies were:
1. Sriman Narayana is supreme
2. The jIvAtmA is different from the paramAtmA
3. Complete surrender is the means to salvation
4. Moksham will be attained by one who has surrendered, at the end of his birth
5. For one who has surrendered, remembrance of the Lord at his deathbed is not necessary
6. Ramanuja should take refuge with Maha Poorna (Periya Nambigal) and take him as his acharya

Thirukkolur Ammal is asking "Did I have the fortune of conversing with the Lord like Thirukkachchi Nambigal did".

Vaarththai 38

38. avan mEni AnEnO thiruppANar pOlE
ந.அ. அவன் மேனி ஆனேனோ திருப்பாணர் போலே

Thiruppanazhvar was born as an ayonija in a field in Uraiyur, near Srirangam. He was picked up by a person from the clan of Pana's (singers) and brought up. A he grew up, he would stand in the banks of Kaveri river, on the other side of Srirangam, with a veena in his hand, singing the praises of Lord Ranganatha. The Lord decided to get him to Srirangam and acted out a play through His brahmin devotee Lokasaranga Muni.

Lokasaranga Muni would go to the banks of Kaveri every day to fetch water for the temple. One time, he saw Thiruppanazhvar there singing. He tried to attract his attention to ask him to move away, but as Azhvar was immersed in singing he did not take notice. So, Lokasarangar threw a stone at him to get his attention. The stone hit Azhvar's head and caused him to bleed. Azhvar then realized what was happening and stepped away. Lokasarangar then returned to Srirangam, where the Lord asked him to apologize to the great devotee Thiruppanazhvar and bring him into Srirangam.

Lokasarangar returned to Azhvar and apologized to him for his conduct and told of the Lord's command to him. When Azhvar refused to set foot in Srirangam, Lokasaranga Muni offered to carry him on his shoulders. As it was the Lord's command, Azhvar could not refuse.

When Lokasarangar brought Azhvar in front of Lord Ranganatha inside the Srirangam temple, Azhvar burst out with the magnificent Amalanadhipiran pasuram, enjoying the divine body of the Lord from feet to the head. At the end of the ten pasurams, Azhvar disappeared from this world and attained the lotus feet of Lord Ranganatha.

Thirukkolur Ammal is asking "Did I become the target of His divine grace and attain His divine feet like Thiruppanazhvar did".

Vaarththai 39

39. anuppi vaiyum enREnO vasishTaraip pOlE

ந கூ. அனுப்பி வையும் என்றேனோ வசிஷ்டரைப் போலே

One time Vishwamitra maharishi came to Dasaratha and asked him to give Rama to help protect the rishi's yaga from the rakshasas who were disturbing it. Dasaratha did not want to send Rama with the rishi, since He was young and Dasaratha could not bear separation
from Him, even though he had promised the rishi anything he wanted. Vishwamitra was not pleased and became angry at Dasaratha. Dasaratha offered to go himself with the rishi but the sage wanted only Rama.

At that time, Vasishta who was the rajaguru of Dasaratha, intervened. Seeing the future with his powers and that Vishwamitra was going to give weapons training as well as great weapons to Rama, he told Dasaratha to send both Rama and Lakshmana with Vishwamitra.

Thirukkolur Ammal is asking "Did I see the benefit for the Lord and ask the father to send his son with the sage, like Vasishta did".

Vaarththai 40

40. aDi vAngkinEnO kongiRpirATTiyaip pOlE

ச0. அடி வாங்கினேனோ கொங்கிற்பிராட்டியைப் போலே

Here, the phrase *'aDi vAngudhal'* refers to requesting and receiving acharya padukas. Kongu Piratti's story is found in Arayirappadi Guru Parampara Prabhavam.

Her original name is Sumathi and she belonged to a town called Kollaikkalam in Kongu desam. One time there was a great famine in the land. So, she and her husband left their town and moved to Srirangam. At Srirangam, she heard and saw the greatness of Swami Ramanuja and the quality of the people who were his disciples. She desired and became one of the devotees of Ramanuja. At that time, she received the name Kongu Piratti (or Kongil Piratti) from him.

After some time, the famine lifted from the land and she desired to return to her home town. She approached Ramanuja, sought his blessings and also obtained his divine padukas for performing thiruvaradhanam.

Several years later, due to the disturbance of the Chola king, Ramanuja had to leave Srirangam and move to

Thirunarayanapuram. On the way, he went through the town where Kongu Piratti was living. She proved to Ramanuja and his disciples that she had a connection to Ramanuja's divine feet by showing them his divine padukas and how she got them. Then she hosted them at her place and made them happy.

Thirukkolur Ammal is asking "Did I have the fortune of receiving acharya padukas like Kongu Piratti did".

Vaarththai 41

41. maN pUvai iTTEnO kuravanambiyaip pOlE

சு.க. மண் பூவை இட்டேனோ குரவநம்பியைப் போலே

Near Thiruppathi was the town of Kuravapuram. Bheeman, an ardent devotee of Lord Srinivasa, lived there. He belonged to the potter class. He created an image of Srinivasa with mud and prayed to Him everyday. Everyday he would make flowers out of mud and present the Lord with them. Our acharyas called this mud flower as 'paNippU'. Srinivasa enjoyed the great love of this devotee.

Due to his great selfless love for the Lord, he came to be called as Kurumbaruththa Nambi; and also as Kuravanambi for his home town. Srinivasa decided that the devotion of Kuravanambi should be brought to the notice of the world. So, when the devoted King Thondaiman presented Him with golden flowers, He showed the mud flowers on top of the golden flowers. Seeing this, the king was surprised. He prayed to the Lord to understand what happened. Srinivasa made him realize the greatness of Kuravanambi. So Thondaiman went to Kuravapuram, met Nambi there and gave him his respects.

It is said that, unable to accept the fact that his private experience with the Lord had become publicized (even by Him), Kuravanambi gave up his life at that moment itself.

Thirukkolur Ammal is asking "Did I pray to the Lord using mud flowers with deep devotion and love like Kuravanambi did".

---

42. mUlam enRu azhaiththEnO gajarAjanaip pOlE

ச உ. மூலம் என்று அழைத்தேனோ கஜராஜனைப் போலே

In the eighth skandam of Bhagavata Puranam, the story of Gajendra the elephant, is written. In the Trikuta mountains, there was a beautiful lotus pond owned by Varuna. One day, a herd of elephants led by Gajendra and his consorts came there. They entered the pond, took a bath and played around. At that time, a crocodile caught the foot of Gajendra. Gajendra fought with all his strength but could not free himself. Later the other elephants too tried to help him but could not. The battle lasted for many years. Eventually, the elephant lost his strength and realized death was imminent. At that time, he also realized that, neither could he save himself nor could he trust other beings. And that the only true refuge was Sriman Narayana. He surrendered to the Lord and called out to the supreme *'namo namaste akhila kAraNAya niShkAraNAya adhbuta kAraNAya'*, and *'AdimUla'* (the one who is the source of all).

Hearing this plea, while every devata stepped aside, Sriman Narayana got on His Garuda and flew to the pond. There, He used His Sudarshana Chakra to cut the head of the crocodile, freed the elephant and protected him. He then personally accepted the flower that the elephant had plucked from the pond for Him.

Gajendra was a king called Indradyumna and the crocodile was a Gandharva called Hoohoo, in their earlier births. Due to a curse, they were born as animals, and now both were freed from their curse. The both praised Sriman Narayana.

This event has been praised greatly by Azhvars and Acharyas in their works.

Thirukkolur Ammal is asking "Did I cry out to the supreme who is the cause for everything and attain His grace like Gajendra did".

---

43. pUsak koDuththEnO kUniyaip pOlE

சங. பூசக் கொடுத்தேனோ கூனியைப் போலே

When Krishna entered Mathura along with Balarama on the invitation of Kamsa through Akrura, He first met a washerman. He and Balarama asked for some new clothes, but the washerman, who worked for Kamsa, refused. So, they defeated him, took some clothes, put them on and left.

Next, they met a florist and accepted fragrant garlands from him (more on this in the next Vaarththai).

Then, as they were walking in the main street, they saw a young and pretty woman who however had a hunchback. In her hand, she was carrying many types of fragrant sandal. Her name was Trivakrai or Naikavakrai.

Krishna looked at her and said "O beautiful girl! Who are you taking this sandal paste for?"

She replied "O beautiful one! I am taking this sandal paste for Kamsa".

Krishna and Balarama asked her for the same sandal paste. She gave them some and they rejected it as being artificially scented. She gave them a different variety and they rejected it as being meant for kings and therefore likely to build arrogance. Pleased that they were able to discern good fragrance from bad, she gave them the sandal paste that matched their divine bodies. They wore it with pleasure.

Then, Krishna placing His foot on her's and two fingers under her chin, lifted her and removed the hunch from her back.

Thirukkolur Ammal is asking "Did I give fragrant paste to the Lord like the hunchback did without thinking about consequences".

Vaarththai 44

44. pUvaik koDuththEnO mAlAkAraraip pOlE

ச ச. பூவைக் கொடுத்தேனோ மாலாகாரரைப் போலே

Krishna and Balarama entered Mathura to take part in the archery event organized by Kamsa. On the way, they met a washerman first. They asked him for some new clothes, but he refused. So, they defeated him, took some clothes, put them on and left. Then they wished to wear new and fragrant flowers. So, they entered a small street and reached the home of a florist. Bhagavatam says that his name was Sudama. Upon seeing them both, Sudama recognized their greatness and fell at their feet.

The two, who looked like freshly blossomed lotuses themselves, asked him for flowers. Sudama praised them and gave them wonderful flowers to wear.

Our acharyas wonder at the fact that a florist who would cover his own face to avoid being attracted to flowers and using them for himself instead of selling them, would give the best garlands that he had, due to the great love he felt for the Lord. Krishna was pleased by the affection shown by the *mAlakAra* and gave him several boons.

Swami Ramanuja praises Sudama along with Akrura in his Gita Bashyam.

It is due to this that many of our Azhvars and Acharyas sought to perform flower service to the Lord.

Thirukkolur Ammal is asking "Did I show the selfless love exhibited by mAlAkAra".

Vaarththai 45

45. vazhi aDimai seydhEnO lakShmaNanaip pOlE

சரு. வழி அடிமை செய்தேனோ லக்ஷ்மணனைப் போலே

When Sri Rama was asked to go to the forest based on the boons that Kaikeyi got from Dasaratha, Lakshmana too wanted to go with Him. Initially, Rama did not agree to that.

Lakshmana pleaded with Rama thus: "Just as a fish would not survive out of the water, so too mother Sita and myself cannot survive separation from You. Therefore, You have to take me with You." He then told Rama that when He and Sita live and play in the sides of mountains, he would perform all kinds of services to them 'aham sarvam karishyAmi'.

Lakshmana's mother Sumitra also told him that he was made for the sake of living in the forest 'srushTstavam vanavAsAya'. She also warned him that he should not lose his mind watching the beauty of Rama's walk and fail in his duties.

Nammazhvar also expresses that only due to Lakshmana following Him, Rama survived in the forest. He worries what might have happened to Him otherwise.

Thirukkolur Ammal is asking "Did I stay with Him always and perform all kinds of services like Lakshmana did".

Vaarththai 46

46. vaiththa iDaththu irundhEnO baradhanaip pOlE

ச சூ. வைத்த இடத்து இருந்தேனோ பரதனைப் போலே

When Kaikeyi asked for the boons of making Bharatha the king and Rama going to the forest for 14 years, Bharatha was not in Ayodhya. He was at his uncle's place in the Kekaya kingdom. After Rama left for the forest and the king Dasaratha died due to separation from Him, the ministers of Ayodhya requested Bharatha to return to Ayodhya. When Bharatha returned and found out what had occured, he became very angry. He then made a decision to get his brother Rama back to Ayodhya and coronate Him as the king.

After the final rites were completed for Dasaratha, Vasishta and the ministers of Ayodhya requested Bharatha to become the king. He refused and said "Both I and this kingdom are the property of Rama. How can one property rule over another?"

He then took his mothers, ministers, pundits, army and a large number of people with him and went into the forest to meet Rama. There, he met Rama, told Him of Dasaratha's demise and prayed to Him "I along with the ministers bow my head to You. Please show mercy on me who is Your brother, disciple and slave".

Rama did not accede. He told Bharatha that they both must fulfill their father's command. He promised Bharatha that He would come back after 14 years in the forest and accept the kingdom, but that Bharatha should rule Ayodhya till that time.

Bharatha agreed, but took Rama's padukas and told Him that he would rule on behalf of the padukas.

Thirukkolur Ammal is asking "Did I show the state of pAratantrya - of accepting the Lord's wish, no matter whether it is agreeable or not - like Bharatha did".

Vaarththai 47

47. akkaraikkE viTTEnO guhapperumALaip pOlE

ச எ. அக்கரைக்கே விட்டேனோ குஹப்பெருமாளைப்
போலே

Following the word of Dasaratha, Sri Rama decided to go to the forest for 14 years. Sumanthra drove Rama, Sita and Lakshmana in a chariot to the banks of Ganges and left them at a town called Srungiberapura. There, the hunters were ruled by Guha. He received Rama with honor and hosted them at his place. Rama spent the night at Guha's place and asked him to take them across the river the next day. Guha took them, as well as their weapons and other items, to the other side of Ganges in a beautiful boat.

Later, when Bharatha and others came to the same place to meet Rama and plead with Him to return, Guha carried them all in 500 boats across the river.

For his noble service to the Lord, Bharatha and their retinue, our elders respectfully refer to Guha as Guha Perumal.

Thirukkolur Ammal is asking "Did I help the Lord and His devotees reach the other side of the river, like Guha did".

Vaarththai 48

48. arakkanuDan porudhEnO periya uDaiyAraip pOlE

சஅ. அரக்கனுடன் பொருதேனோ பெரிய உடையாரைப் போலே

When Sri Rama, Sita and Lakshmana left sage Agastya's ashrama for Panachavati, on the way they met an old vulture.

When they asked who he was, the vulture replied "My name is Jatayu and I am your father Dasaratha's friend." Rama bowed to the vulture and enquired about him and his antecedents.

Jatayu replied "One of the wives of Kashyapa Prajapati was Thamra. In her clan was born Vinata. Vinata had two sons Garuda and Aruna. To Aruna were born two sons - the elder is Sambhati and I am the younger, Jatayu. I am living in this forest and I will accompany You while You are here", and blessed them.

So, Rama, Sita, Lakshmana and Jatayu all went together to Panchavati. Jatayu stayed close to the ashrama where Rama was staying. Rama told Lakshmana "We have been separated from our father. So, let's stay under the wings of Jatayu".

Later, Ravana planned to abduct Sita and used Mareecha to trick Rama and Lakshmana, and get them away from Her. As he was carrying away Sita, Jatayu intercepted them. He tried to talk Ravana into giving up this bad idea and release Sita. When he did not listen, Jatayu began waging a great war with Ravana. He broke Ravana's chariot and attacked him fiercely. In the end, Ravana managed to cut Jatayu's wings and feet and threw him to the ground. He then left with Sita to Lanka.

When Rama and Lakshmana came looking for Sita, they saw Jatayu lying on the ground. Jatayu told them what happened, performed mangalashasana to Rama by calling Him *'Ayushman'* and then gave up his life. Due to that and the great respect Rama had for him, our acharyas refer to Jatayu as Periya Udaiyar.

Thirukkolur Ammal is asking "Did I fight with Ravana and dare to give up my body and soul, like Periya Udaiyar did".

---

49. ikkaraikkE senREnO vibIshaNanaip pOlE

சக. இக்கரைக்கே சென்றேனோ விபீஷ்ணனைப் போலே

After Hanuman discovered the presence of Sita in Lanka, Rama came to the opposite shore from Lanka, with a huge monkey army under the guidance of Sugreeva. At that time, Ravana called a meeting in his rajya sabha and discussed the situation. His ministers and army leaders told him that their army would easily defeat the army of Rama and Sugreeva. They said "With Ravana and Indrajit, who defeated even the devas under Indra, on our side, how could we lose to a mere army of men and monkeys?"

The only one in the meeting who objected was Ravana's brother Vibeeshana. He said "It is not smart to judge another army without fully judging its capability. From the time Sita was kidnapped and brought here, we have been seeing many inauspicious signs. Sita is a great pativrata. Rama and Lakshmana are incomparable warriors. At Janastana, Rama destroyed our huge army in no time, by Himself. They have also killed rakshasas such as Virata and Kabanda. Therefore, it is best that we return Sita to Rama and discuss peace. That's our only path to survival. I am saying this because of my interest in what is best for our clan."

Ravana and Indrajit were not pleased with this talk and they abused Vibeeshana. When Vibeeshana insisted again, Ravana got angry with him and asked him to leave Lanka.

Vibeeshana left Lanka along with four of his close friends and flew across the ocean to where Rama and His army were camped. There, he sought surrender at Rama's divine feet, the *sarva loka sharaNya*. Initially, Sugreeva and others objected to accepting Vibeeshana. Rama, however, disagreed and accepted Vibeeshana, who fell at His feet and said "I have given up all my prior attachments. My life is now entirely in Your hands."

Thirukkolur Ammal is asking "Did I leave everything on this side and go to where the Lord is, like Vibeeshana did".

Vaarththai 50

50. iniyadhu enRu vaiththEnO sabariyaip pOlE

௫0. இனியது என்று வைத்தேனோ சபரியைப் போலே

In the ashrama of Mathanga rishi lived a woman called Sabari, who belonged to the hunter tribe. She served the rishi and his disciples and became the target of their grace. When they attained siddhi and left for the higher worlds, she wanted to go with them.

However, Mathanga rishi told her "Sri Rama and Lakshmana will be coming to this area in the future. You should serve and worship them and by their grace you can reach us".

Obeying her acharya's words, Sabari stayed back looking forward to the arrival of Rama and Lakshmana.

Due to the greatness of Mathanga rishi, in the forest near his ashrama, plucked flowers would not wilt and plucked fruits would not age or lose their good taste. Sabari collected the fruits, tested them herself for sweetness and kept them for Rama.

After the abduction of Sita, Rama and Lakshmana went in search of Her. On the way, they met and killed a rakshasa called Kabandha (see Vaarththai 17). Before he died, Kabandha told them to meet and gain the friendship of Sugreeva. He also told them to see Sabari, at the ashrama of Mathanga muni.

So, Rama and Lakshmana came to the ashrama of Mathanga and met her there. She prayed to them and offered them the fruits that she had gathered and kept for them. Due to her pure devotion, Rama accepted her service. In turn, she lost her sins and attained the fruits of her acharya bhakti.

Thirukkolur Ammal is asking "Did I offer sweet fruits to the Lord, like Sabari did".

Vaarththai 51

51. ingkum uNDu enREnO prahlAdhanaip pOlE

ரு க. இங்கும் உண்டு என்றேனோ ப்ரஹ்லாதனைப் போலே

The asuras Hiranyaksha and Hiranyakashipu were brothers. They both were very cruel. Hiranyaksha hid the world under the ocean and Sriman Narayana took the Varaha avatara to restore it. After doing that, He killed Hiranyaksha.

Due to that, Hiranyakashpu developed hatred toward Him. He performed great penance to Brahma, obtained several boons from him and started ruling this world and Indraloka. He then put forth the command that no one should worship Sriman Narayana and that everyone should worship him instead.

Prahlada was the son of Hiranyakashipu. Despite being born to this evil asura, Prahlada was a great devotee of Sriman Narayana. While the teachers of Hiranyakashipu's land taught all children that Hiranya was the supreme power, Prahlada prayed only to Narayana and also taught the same to the children in his gurukula.

This infuriated Hiranya and he began many attempts at torturing and even killing Prahlada: such as using weapons, having poisonous snakes bite him, crushing him with elephants, throwing him from a mountain-top, throwing him in fire, throwing him into the ocean, etc. Prahlada's mind was always set on Narayana and as such Hiranya was unable to do anything to him.

In spite of everything that Hiranya did to him, Prahlada showed no anger toward him. Instead he advised Hiranya "Vishnu is the antaryami to everything in this universe. Being that the case, where is the idea of considering some as friends and some as enemies. Just as He is inside me, so too He is inside you. He is present everywhere."

At that time, Hiranya showed a pillar and asked Prahlada if He was in it. Prahlada answered that He was everywhere including inside that pillar. When Hiranya wrecked that pillar, Sriman Narayana appeared as Narasimha and killed Hiranya by ripping him with his finger nails.

Nammazhvar celebrates this event:
engkum uLan kaNNan enRa maganayk kAyndhu
ingku illaiyAl enRu iraNiyan thUN puDaippa
angku appozhudhE avan vIyath thOnRiya en
singkap pirAn perumai ArAyum sIrmaiththE

Thirukkolur Ammal is asking "Did I say with great conviction that He is everywhere including here (in this pillar), like Prahlada did".

Vaarththai 52

52. ingku illai enREnO dhadhipANDanaip pOlE

ரு உ. இங்கு இல்லை என்றேனோ ததிபாண்டனைப்
போலே

The name Dhadhipanda means one who has a large yogurt pot. Each day, Dhadhipanda would take a large pot of yogurt and go about selling it. In the evening, he would come back with the empty pot and rest outside his home.

One day, Krishna was sitting in his mother Yashoda's lap and drinking milk. Suddenly she remembered leaving milk on the stove and she left Krishna and ran inside to take the milk out before it got overheated. Krishna became angry at that and threw a stone on a pot containing ghee. When Yashoda returned, she saw the broken ghee pot while Krishna sat innocently nearby. She became angry at Him and called out to Him while brandishing a small stick. Krishna began to run crying and Yashoda started to run behind Him.

While running to escape His mother, Krishna saw Dhadhipanda and his pot. So, he told him "O Dhadhipanda! My mother is angry with me and she is going to hit me. Please hide me in your pot and tell her that you did not see me". So, Dhadhipanda hid Krishna in his pot. When Yashoda came there and asked if he had seen Krishna and if He was hiding there, he lied by saying "He is not here".

Believing him, Yashoda left. Krishna then called out from inside the pot "O Dhadhipanda! I am not able to breathe inside here. Please let me out".

Dhadhipanda was graced at that time by the Lord and he realized that Krishna was the supreme.

So, he told Krishna "O Krishna! Only if You promise to give me moksha, will I let you out".

After a short argument Krishna agreed. Not satisfied, Dhadhipanda also asked for moksha for his pot and Krishna acquiesced. As promised, Krishna gave moksha to both Dhadhipanda and his pot.

No one can say, upon whom the Lord's grace would fall. In the previous Vaarththai, one saw that His grace fell on Prahlada who told that He was everywhere. In this Vaarththai, it is seen that He gave moksha to Dhadhipanda who said that He was not there (he had not seen him).

Thirukkolur Ammal is asking "Did I say a lie (that He was not present nearby) for His sake, like Dhadhipanda did".

---

53. kATTukkup pOnEnO perumALaip pOlE

ரு ங. காட்டுக்குப் போனேனோ பெருமாளைப் போலே

After Dasaratha decided to coronate Rama as the king, he informed everyone in his kingdom and with the consultations of his gurus set a date for the event.

The night before the coronation ceremony, Rama performed a vratam along with Sita and prayed to Lord Ranganatha. However, due to the ill advise of Mantara, Kaikeyi had a change of heart and demanded two boons that she had from Dasaratha. With those boons, she asked that her son Bharatha be crowned the king instead of Rama and that Rama should go to the forest for 14 years.

Hearing that Dasaratha became extremely sad and fainted. When Rama came to the palace of Kaikeyi, she told Him about the two boons and that it was a royal decree that He go to the forest.

Rama immediately accepted it and with great pleasure prepared to go to the forest.

Thirukkolur Ammal is asking "Did I show steadiness in my heart and mind like Rama showed in following His father's word, gave up the kingdom and went to the forest".

Vaarththai 54

54. kaNDu vandhEn enREnO thiruvaDiyaip pOlE

ரு ச. கண்டு வந்தேன் என்றேனோ திருவடியைப் போலே

When Rama and Lakshmana went in search of the abducted Sita, on the way they met Kabandha and killed him. Before dying, Kabandha told them that they should meet with Sugreeva and make friendship with him; and that he would help them in their search for Sita. They did the same and helped Sugreeva become the king of the vanara kingdom.

Sugreeva then sent monkeys in the four directions to find the place where Sita had been kept. In the southern direction went Angada, Jambavan and Hanuman (*siRiya thiruvaDi*). Knowing that it would be Hanuman that would find Sita, Rama had given him a ring to show to Her, to prove that he was indeed the messenger of Rama.

Learning from Jatayu's brother Sambhati that Sita was kept in Lanka, Hanuman was selected by the vanaras to leap across the ocean and meet with Her. Meeting Sita in Lanka, Hanuman showed Her the ring from Rama, gave His message and made Her feel better.

Returning to Rama, he told Him that he had seen Sita ('*drushTA sItA*'). He also gave Rama the head ornament ('chUDAmaNi') from Sita that She had given him. Seeing the ornament and hearing the message, Rama became very pleased and embraced Hanuman.

This selfless service by Hanuman is greatly praised by our acharyas.

Thirukkolur Ammal is asking "Did I do service to the Lord, like Hanuman did".

Vaarththai 55

55. iru kaiyum viTTEnO dhraupadhiyaip pOlE

ரு ரு. இரு கையும் விட்டேனோ த்ரௌபதியைப் போலே

Due to their jealousy of the Pandavas, Duryodhana and the Kauravas, under the advice of their uncle Sakuni, invited them to a game of dice. In that game, they defeated the Pandavas using Sakuni's unfair mean and took over their kingdom, all their wealth and enslaved them. Finally, they made Yudishtra pledge Draupadi in the game and won her as well.

Wishing to insult them, they made Duschasana drag her to the court even though she was in need of privacy at that time. This ended in the decision to attempt to disrobe her in public, which Dushcasana began to carry out.

When she cried out for help, no one in the sabha, including Bheeshma, Drona and even the Pandavas, came to her aid. At that time, she remembered the sage Vasishta's words that Narayana is the sole refuge and surrendered to Him with both hands raised over her head and saying:

shanka chakra gadApANe dvArakanilayAchyuta!
govinda! puNDarIkAksha! rakshamAm sharaNAgatam

Realizing that she can neither depend on her own self nor on others for her protection, she performed complete surrender to the Lord. It is next to impossible for a woman to give up her natural sense of modesty and let go of her dress in a public place. Such was her faith in Krishna. At that time, Sri Krishna was in Dwaraka. And from there itself, He made her dress grow, thereby tiring Duschasana and making him give up.

Thirukkolur Ammal is asking "Did I show complete faith in the Lord, like Draupadi, who lifted both hands and took refuge in Him, did".

Vaarththai 56

56. ingku pAl pongkum enREnO vaDuganambiyaip pOlE

ரு.சு. இங்கு பால் பொங்கும் என்றேனோ வடுகநம்பியைப் போலே

Vaduga Nambi (Andra Poorna) was one of the close disciples of Swami Ramanuja. His faith in his acharya was unshakeable and superceded even bhagavad bhakti. This is known as Madhurakavi nishtai (also known as Charamopaya nishtai) - the acharya bhakti shown by Madhurakavi Azhvar toward his acharya Nammazhvar.

It is said that he would call Mudhaliyandan and Kooraththazhvan as *'iru karaiyar'* - meaning that they believe in both their acharya and the Lord. His approach was that, one should place their faith completely in one's acharya alone (as both the means and the end) and no one else.

One time while he was engaged in preparing milk for Ramanuja at Srirangam, Namperumal's thiruveedhi procession was occuring. As Namperumal came outside Ramanuja's mutt, everyone went out to have His darshan. Ramanuja was outside and noticing Vaduga Nambi's absence called him to come outside. Vaduga

Nambi refused saying that if he stepped out, then the milk he was preparing for Ramanuja would overheat, overflow and lose its flavor. Such was his acharya bhakti.

Thirukkolur Ammal is asking "Did I show the kind of acharya bhakti that Vaduga Nambi did".

---

57. iru miDaRu piDiththEnO selvappiLLaiyaip pOlE

ரு எ. இரு மிடறு பிடித்தேனோ செல்வப்பிள்ளையைப்
போலே

Due to the problems created by the shaivite Chola king, Ramanuja had to leave Srirangam. He then went to Karnataka to the Hoysala rajya. There he found that he did not have any more divine mud to wear the Urdhva Pundra. As he was wondering what to do, Lord Thirunarayana appeared in his dream and told him to go to Yadavadri.

He said "Yadavadri is no longer inhabited and I am buried under a mud hill. Find me from the ground, install me in a temple and perform thiruvardhanam. You will also find the divine mud in Yadavadri for Urdhva pundra".

Ramanuja took the help of the Hoysala king, discovered Thirunarayana Perumal and performed thiruvaradhanam for Him for three days. However, as they were not able to find the utsava vigraha, he was sad.

Again, Thirunarayana appeared in his dream and told him "Our utsava murthi, Ramapriyar, is with the daughter of the padsha at Delhi. Go there and bring Him back here".

Ramanuja, therefore, left for Delhi. There he met the padsha, blessed him and asked him to return Ramapriyar. The king said that if Ramanuja invited Him and He responded, then he could take Him back. So Ramanuja invited Him, like Periyazhvar called to Krishna in his divine pasurams *'sArngapANi thaLar nadai nadavAnO'*.

Ramapriyar responded and walked with all His jewels ringing, to Ramanuja and sat in his lap. Ramanuja embraced Him and called Him *'vArAy! en selvappiLLaiyE!'* ('Come my dear child'). Ramapriyar also embraced Ramanuja by wrapping His divine hands around his neck. From that day forward, He was called *'selvappiLLai'* and *'yatirAja sampat kumAra'*. Ramanuja then returned to Yadavadri with Selva Pillai and installed Him in the temple and performed utsavams for Him.

Thirukkolur Ammal is asking "Did I embrace the acharya like Selva Pillai did".

Vaarththai 58

58. nil enRu peRREnO iDaiyARRUr nambiyaip pOlE

ரு.அ. நில் என்று பெற்றேனோ இடையாற்றூர் நம்பியைப்
போலே

In our sampradhayam, the anticipation of the devotees to experience the Lord is greatly praised. Nammazhvar in his thiruvaymozhi pasuram 7-10-4 says 'kaNNapirAn than idaiyamalaraDip pOdhugaLE eppOdhum manaththu Ingku ninaigap peRa vAykkum kol'. We also see the great anticipation that Akrura showed on his way to meet Krishna.

There is an event related to this that is shown in *EeDu* vyakhyanam.

At Srirangam, the Lord enjoys four brahmotsavams each year. A devotee from Idaiyatrukudi called *idaiyARRUr nambi* would come to every utsavam on the first day itself (*angurArppaNam*) and attend till the last day. After he returned home, he would keep thinking of nothing but the utsavam. This was both his sustenance and pleasure. If someone told him that it was time to eat, he would ask in reply whether the next utsavam has neared.

When he became 100 years old, due to old age he lost his strength. During one brahmotsavam, he was unable to go to Srirangam on the first day itself. As such, he made it there only on the sixth day.

Meanwhile, seeing that His devotee was not there on day one, Namperumal wondered "Idaiyatru Nambi has not made it to the first day of our utsavam". Seeing him on the sixth day, Nameprumal became very happy and told him "I would like to give you a boon".

Nambi did not ask Him anything. Instead he mentioned "Through the body You gave me, I worshipped for these many years. Now that old age has come, this body is no longer capable of travel".

Namperumal replied "From now on, stay here itself" (just as he had told Ramanuja to stay at Srirangam – 'atraiva srIrange sukhamAsva').

And as Namperumal reached the next street in procession, Nambi left this world and reached His divine abode.

Thirukkolur Ammal is asking "Did I worship Him and think about nothing else like Idaiyatru Nambi did and was told by Namperumal to stay at His place".

---

59. neDundhUram pOnEnO nAthamuniyaip pOlE

ரு.கூ. நெடுந்தூரம் போனேனோ நாதமுனியைப் போலே

Nathamunigal's original name was Ranganathamishrar. He is the primary acharya in Srivaishnava sampradhayam after Perumal, Thayar, Vishvaksenar and Nammazhvar. He is celebrated by Kooraththazhvan in his guru paramparai thaniyan *'lakshmInAtha samArambhAm nAtha yAmuna madhyamAm'*.

It was through his great effort that the 4000 divya prabandha verses that were lost were obtained. Nathamunigal was a great exponent of the Ashtanga Yoga. He used that to meditate on Nammazhvar in Azhvar Thirunagari and obtained the Divya Prabandham from Azhvar.

He saw the Lord in everything in this world. One time, while he was in yoga, a Chola king came to his place with the women of his household to see him. After he left, Nathamunigal heard about the incident. He then left behind the king and walked all the way to the capital city of Gangai Konda Chozhapuram. His disciples followed him and met him there. They asked him why he had followed the king. Nathamunigal replied "I saw them as Sri Krishna and His gopikas and that's why I followed them". This is the state described by Nammazhvar as *'thiruvuDai mannaraik kANil thirumAlaik kaNDEnE ennum'*.

Another time, Nathamunigal was deep in meditation. When he came out of it, the people in his household told him that two men who catch and train animals, a woman and a monkey came to see him and left. Nathamunigal replied "They must be Sri Rama, Lakshmana, Sita and Hanuman" and started heading in the direction that they went.

As he went, he asked the people in the way if they had seen this group. They agreed and so he followed them all the way to Gangai Konda Chozhapuram. There when he made his enquiries about the group, people told him that they had not seen any such group. Hearing that, Nathamunigal became extremely sad, collapsed there itself and left for His abode.

Thirukkolur Ammal is asking "Did I walk a long distance looking for the Lord, like Nathamunigal did".

Vaarththai 60

60. avan pOnAn enREnO mAruthiyANDAn pOlE

சூ0. அவன் போனான் என்றேனோ மாருதியாண்டான்
போலே

Because of the troubles created by the Chola king, Ramanuja moved to Thirunarayanapuram in Karnataka and lived there for many years (see Vaarththai 57). While he was there, he would often remember Srirangam and Kooraththazhvan and missing them both, would long for his return.

This chola king is called 'avyapadeshya' by Srivaishnava acharyas - that is, one who is not worthy of being called by his name. He later died due to a festering wound in his neck and so was also refered to as 'kirumi kaNDan'.

Ramanuja had a disciple called 'mARenRillA mAruthi siRiyANDAn' or 'mAruthiyANDAn'. He called this disciple and told him to visit Srirangam and bring back news about the temple, Kooraththazhvan, Periya Nambigal and others. Maruthiyandan went to Srirangam and gave the news about Ramanuja to those there. He also heard about Periya Nambigal attaining the Lord's lotus feet and Azhvan losing his eyes and became very sad. At that time, he also heard about the king's death. He became happy on hearing this news (as it meant Ramanuja could return to Srirangam) and walked very quickly back to Thirunarayanapuram.

At Thirunarayanapuram, he met Ramanuja and said *'avan pOnAn'*, meaning that the chola king was dead. Hearing that, Ramanuja too became happy that he could now go back to Srirangam and embraced Maruthiyandan and another disciple Ammangi Ammal who had gone with him. However, he too became very sad on hearing the news about Kooraththazhvan and Periya Nambigal. Afterward, he consoled himself and returned to Srirangam.

Thirukkolur Ammal is asking "Did I walk a long distance and give good news to the acharya like Maruthiyandan did".

Vaarththai 61

61. avan vENDAm enREnO AzhvAnaip pOlE

சூ க. அவன் வேண்டாம் என்றேனோ ஆழ்வானைப்
போலே

Due to the trouble caused by the Chola king, Ramanuja had left Srirangam for Thirunarayanapuram. Periya Nambigal had given up his life and Koorathathazhvan lost his eyesight. After performing the final rites for Periya Nambigal, Koorathathazhvan returned to Srirangam.

One time, unable to bear the separation from Ramanuja, Koorathathazhvan was in deep despair. To console himself, he went to the Srirangam temple. However, due to his anger against Ramanuja, the Chola king had decreed that no one who was associated with Ramanuja should be allowed inside the temple. Therefore, a gatekeeper at the temple stopped Azhvan from entering. Another gatekeeper said "Even though Azhvan is associated with Ramanuja, he is full of good qualities. Therefore, he can be allowed inside", and told Azhvan that he could go in.

Azhvan replied "I should be allowed to see the Lord because of my relationship with my acharya and not because I have good qualities. Seeing the Lord while breaking connection with one's acharya is not required". Saying so, he refused to go inside the temple and went back.

Thirukkolur Ammal is saying "Did I show interest in the relationship to my acharya to the extent of saying no to even Sriman Narayana, like Kooraththazhvan did".

Vaarththai 62

62. advaitam venREnO emperumAnAraip pOlE

சூ உ. அத்வைதம் வென்றேனோ எம்பெருமானாரைப்
போலே

In explaining the meanings of the Vedas and Vedantas, three major sampradhayams came into being - Advaitam, Visishtadvaitam and Dvaitam. In these, Advaitam says that the Supreme Lord alone is the truth and that everything else is false. Even though the jIva may appear to be different based on our experiences, it is not different from the supreme. This is the interpretation of Adi Shankara of the famous Upanishad statement *'tat tvam asi'*. Dvaitam says that the Supreme and the jIva are always different and separate.

In the Vedantas, one can see statements that support the former (*abheda sruti*) and the latter (*bheda sruti*). Swami Ramanuja followed the teachings of Alavandar, poorvacharyas and the words of Azhvars and established Visishtadvaitam based on both bheda and abheda srutis. The cornerstone of this sampradhayam is the *sharIrAtma bhAva* between the Supreme and the jIva – that is, the Supreme acts as the antaryami of all souls (*'yasya AtmA sharIram'*). Azhvar establishes this as *'uDal misai uyir enak karandhu engum parandhu uLan'*.

Vedas too say the same as *'antarbahischa tat sarvam vyApya nArAyaNa sthita:'*.

In his work Sri Bhashya, which is a commentary to the Brahma Sutra, Ramanuja condemns the *mAyA vAdam* of the advaita sampradhayam. This is celebrated in Dhati Panchakam as *'mAyAvAdi bhujanga bhanga garuDa'* and by Amudhanar in Ramanuja Nutrandhadhi as *'uyirgaL meyviTTu AdhipparanODu onRAm enRu sollum avvallal ellAm vAdhil venRAn'*.

Even when he was a student and learning from the advaita teacher Yadavaprakasha, he had the courage to correct the statements made by him. Later, he debated the great advaita vidwan Yajnamurthi, defeated him and took him as his disciple (he would be renamed as Arulala Perumal Emberumanar).

Thirukkolur Ammal is saying "Did I challenge and win the well established siddhantam of Advaitam like Ramanuja did".

In this word by Thirukkolur Ammal, an interesting feature is that, it is addressed to Ramanuja and it is about Ramanuja - that is, she speaks to Ramanuja about him in the third person.

Vaarththai 63

63. aruLAzhi kaNDEnO nallAnaip pOlE

சூ நி. அருளாழி கண்டேனோ நல்லானைப் போலே

In the banks of Kaveri river in a town lived a brahmin devotee of Sriman Narayana. One time during floods, a dead body was washed ashore. The brahmin saw the marks of Shanka and Chakra on the shoulders of the body and realized that it was that of a Srivaishnava. Therefore, without examining further to determine who it might have been, what caste he might have belonged to, etc, he performed the final rites for that person.

The people in the town were not pleased with what happened. They said that the body was that of a low caste person and that this brahmin should not have performed final rites for him. Therefore, they made him an outcast. The brahmin prayed to the Lord to correct the townsfolk.

The next day at the temple in the town where the town people were gathered, the Lord spoke through the priest and told them "You may not find the brahmin devotee acceptable. But to Me, he is a good person ('nallAn'). Therefore, you too should accept him as such". From that day forward, he and his descendants came to be known as 'Nallan Chakravarthy'.

The Lord's Chakra (discus) is also known as 'aruL Azhi'. Nallan saw only the mark of the 'aruLAzhi' and nothing else. In the process, he also saw the depth of the Lord's grace (*'aruL Azham'*).

Thirukkolur Ammal is asking "Did I see only the mark of the Lord's discus and nothing else, like Nallan did".

Vaarththai 64

64. ananthapuram pukkEnO ALavandhAraip pOlE

சூ ச. அனந்தபுரம் புக்கேனோ ஆளவந்தாரைப் போலே

Alavandar, the grandson of Nathamunigal, was the leader of Srivaishnavas at Srirangam and having taken sanyashrama dharma lived in his mutt there. He was performing service to the Lord as the darshana pravarthaka.

One day, while he was at the temple, Thiruvaranga Perumal Araiyar was reciting Nammazhvar's Thiruvaymozhi with both music and abhinaya (dramatic action). As he sang *'kedum iDar AyavellAm'*, the phrase *'kaDuvinai kaLaiyalAgum ... ezhil aNi ananthapuram ... naDaminO namaragaL uLLIr'* occured. Araiyar Swami looked at Alavandar's face and repeated *'naDaminO'* three times.

Understanding the Lord's command through Araiyar, that he should go to Thiruvananthapuram and serve the Lord there per Azhvar's words, Alavandar took the permission of Namperumal. He then asked one of his disciples, Dheyvariyandan, to take care of his mutt and headed immediately to Thiruvananthapuram. There he performed service to the Lord and stayed for a while before his return to Srirangam.

It was during this stay that he missed meeting Kurugai Kavalappan, the disciple of Nathamunigal, to whom Nathamunigal had taught yoga rahasya and told him to pass it on to Alavandar.

Thirukkolur Ammal is asking "Did I understand the Lord's wish and go to Thiruvananthapuram, like Alavandar did".

Vaarththai 65

65. Ariyanaip pirindhEnO dheyvAriyANDAn pOlE

சூ.ரு. ஆரியனைப் பிரிந்தேனோ தெய்வாரியாண்டான்
போலே

When Alavandar left for Thiruvananthapuram (see previous Vaarththai), he left his mutt at Srirangam under the care of his disciple, Dheyvariyandan. Dheyvariyandan did not want to be separated from his acharya. However, as it was the word of his acharya, he stayed back and started taking care of the mutt. The separation was too much to bear for him though and his health started deteriorating. The other disciples at the mutt began to worry about him and had a physician take a look at his health. The physician told them that it was his mental state that was affected due to the separation from his acharya which in turn was affecting his physical health.

The disciples decided that he would not survive being separated from Alavandar and decided to take him to Thiruvananthapuram. As he was too weak to walk, they placed him in a chair and began carrying him. As they got closer and closer to Thiruvananthapuram, Andan became happier and happier and as such his health began to pick up. Soon he became healthy enough to walk and started doing so.

At the same time, Alavandar too began his return journey to Srirangam. The two met on the way and Andan fell at the feet of his acharya. Alavandar remarked "Sri Rama told Bharata to stay back at Ayodhya for 14 years. Rama being supremely independent and powerful, Bharata followed His word and stayed there. Since I am neither, Andan has come here now".

Andan felt very bad and stayed on the ground. Alavandar then said "Are you going to stay down till I too become independent?" Fearing anything more being said, Andan came up and stood quietly.

The other disciples then told Alavandar what had happened. Hearing that Alavandar became happy and told Andan "You have lost so much weight. Go and pray to the Lord at Thiruvananthapuram and come back".

Andan replied "When my Thiruvananthapuram is standing in front of me (meaning Alavandar), why do I need to go to another Thiruvananthapuram?" and fell at his acharya's feet again.

Alavandar appreciated his acharya bhakti and returned to Srirangam with him and the other disciples.

Thirukkolur Ammal is asking "Did I separate from my acharya and almost lose my life, like Dheyvariyandan did".

---

66. andhAdhi sonnEnO amudhanAraip pOlE

சு. சு. அந்தாதி சொன்னேனோ அமுதனாரைப் போலே

During Ramanuja's time at Srirangam, there was a great scholar there called Periya Koyil Nambi who held a high office at the temple. Initially he was antagonistic to Ramanuja. Ramanuja corrected him through Kooraththazhvan and he became the disciple of Azhvan. He then developed great devotion toward Ramanuja. Since he was capable of writing wonderful and sweet poems, he was also called as 'Amudhanar' (also Thiruvarangaththamudhanar).

One time he wrote a few verses praising Ramanuja to a great extent and submitted them to Ramanuja. Ramanuja rejected them and threw them away saying that those verses were not appropriate.

He then told Amudhanar "If you still wish to write verses about us, write about our great affinity to the divyadesams, Azhvars, our acharyas such as Nathamunigal and Alavandar and your acharya Kooraththazhvan".

Amudhanar therefore wrote the famous Ramanuja Nutrandhadhi pasurams - 108 pasuram in andhadhi style, in which each pasuram uses the word Ramanuja while showing Ramanuja's affinity to divyadesams, Azhvars and Acharyas.

In one verse, Amudhanar also included the greatness of his acharya Kooraththazhvan (*'mozhiyaik kaDakkum perum pugazhAn'*).

When Ramanuja heard this work, he approved it and it was determined that this work would become part of the daily recitation (*nityAnusandAnam*) for all Srivaishnavas. This work is included at the end of the Azhvar's divya prabandham and is now part of the 4000 verses.

Thirukkolur Ammal is asking "Did I write nectar like verses on my acharya, like Amudhanar did".

---

67. anukUlam sonnEnO mAlyavAnaip pOlE

சூ எ. அனுகூலம் சொன்னேனோ மால்யவானைப் போலே

There were many people who gave good advice to Ravana, such as Maricha, Sita Piratti, Vibeeshana, Kumbakarna and Malyavan, though he did not listen to them. Malyavan was Ravana's grandfather. Due to his age, relationship, knowledge and worldly experience, he was in the right position to offer his advice to Ravana.

He told Ravana "O King! You should not go to war with Rama without knowing His strength. Amongst the boons you received, you never got one that protects you against men or monkeys. Now, both are standing together against you. In addition, this Rama does not appear to be an ordinary human being. It is Lord Vishnu Himself who has incarnated as Rama. Our entire clan will be destroyed in this war. So, return Sita to Rama and make peace with Him". Ravana however, rejected this good advice.

Thirukkolur Ammal is asking "Did I give words of good advice (that show the right path), like Malyavan did".

68. kaLvan ivan enREnO lOkaguruvaip pOlE

சூ.அ. கள்வன் இவன் என்றேனோ லோககுருவைப் போலே

The name *'kaLvan'* is one of the many names of Sriman Narayana. He is known by that name in one His divyadesams as well. It means, one who steals or one who tricks others. He does this for the sake of His devotees in many cases.

In the yagasala of Mahabali, He arrived in the form of a small dwarf (*vAmana*), asked for and obtained three steps of land, grew up as Trivikrama and measured all the worlds with His divine feet. At that time, the asura guru, Sukracharya called Him as a *'kaLvan'*. However, it does not appear appropriate that this is the incident being refered to in this Vaarththai and that Sukracharya is being called a Loka Guru.

It would be appropriate to refer to Swami Nammazhvar as Loka Guru. In several pasurams, Nammazhvar refers to the Lord as *'kaLvan'*. In Thiruvaymozhi, he says *'kaLLa vEDaththaik koNDu pOyp puram pukkavARum'* - here he refers to the Lord going amidst the asuras and taking away their faith in the Vedas. He also says *'koLvan nAn mAvali mUvaDi thA enRa kaLvanE'*, refering to the Lord's vAmana avatara.

In another place, Azhvar says *'kaLvA! emmaiyum Ezulagum nin uLLE thORRiya iRaiva'* In this pasuram, it is Shiva who calls the Lord *'kaLvan'*. This refers to the incident where Shiva obtained a boon from Narayana that He would ask for and get a boon from him. To fulfill that promise, during His Krishna avatara, He went on a kailasha yatra and asked Shiva to grant Him children. Shiva calls Him *'kaLvan'* because, it is He who is the father of all including Shiva and yet He is asking him for the boon of a child. Since Shiva is known for the greatness of his knowledge it would be alright that he is referred to as the Loka Guru.

Thirumangai Azhvar in his Thirunedunthandagam, says *'kArvAnaththu uLLAy! kaLvA!'*. Azhvar says it is His trickery in hiding and not showing Himself to Azhvar. At another place in Thirunedunthandagam, Azhvar says *'puLLUrum kaLvA! nI pOgEl'*. Since this Azhvar invited the Lord Himself to learn from him *'kaNNa, nin thanakkum kuRippAgil kaRkalAm kaviyin poruL'*, it would be appropriate to refer to him as Loka Guru.

Thirukkolur Ammal is asking "Did I refer to Him as *'kaLvan'* like the knowledgeable devotees who can be called as Loka Gurus".

---

69. kaDalOsai enREnO periyanambiyaip pOlE

சூ.சூ. கடலோசை என்றேனோ பெரியநம்பியைப் போலே

One of Alavandar's disciples was Maraneri Nambi who was born in a low caste. He was the target of Alavandar's grace. Another disciple of Alavandar, Periya Nambi, who was the acharya of Swami Ramanuja, had great affection for him as well. Because he had understood the true nature of his soul, Maraneri Nambi separated from his relatives who did not understand him and lived alone. After Alavandar ascended to His divine abode, Maraneri Nambi became physically sick and was struggling. Periya Nambi took him under his care without looking at their caste difference, and gave him food from his own home.

When Maraneri Nambi was in his final stages of his life, he asked Periya Nambi that his body not be given back to his relatives for final rites. He told Periya Nambi *'purODAsaththai nAykkiDAdhE nOkki aruLa vENum'* – that is, do not give the offering meant for devas to dogs. After Maraneri Nambi left this world, Periya Nambi followed his words and performed all the final rites for him, standing in his son's stead. Many brahmins became very upset that an acharya and brahmin such as Periya

Nambi performed final rites for a low caste person and refused to interact with him.

At that time, Ramanuja talked to Periya Nambi and requested to him "When there are many others who could have done these final rites, did you have to do them yourself? Now so many are disrespecting you".

Periya Nambi replied "Come, O Ramanuja! Am I greater than He who was born in the Ikshvaku family and lived as Dharma itself; and is Maraneri Nambi any less than Periya Udaiyar? Am I greater than Dharmaputra; and is Maraneri Nambi any less than Vidhura?"

Periya Nambi refered to the fact that Sri Rama had performed the final rites for a vulture (Jatayu) and that Yudishtra had performed final rites for a low caste person Vidhura.

He added "Do we ask someone else to do our sandhyavandanam?". This was to answer Ramanuja's question as to why he could not have had someone else do the final rites.

He also said "Are the words of Nammazhvar in the pasurams Payilum Sudaroli and Nedumarkkadimai nothing more than noise made by the ocean? Are these something that I have to explain and you have to understand?".

These two decads of Thiruvaymozhi speak of the greatness of bhAgavatas. Periya Nambi was asking if Azhvar's words were not to be actually followed in real life and were empty like the noise of the ocean. Guru Paramparai records that Ramanuja immediately acceded to Periya Nambi's words.

Thirukkolur Ammal is asking "Did I do great bhAgavata service and not treat Azhvar's words like mere noise, like Periya Nambi did".

This episode is also interesting, since Thirukkolur Ammal _is reminding Ramanuja of the words spoken by Periya Nambi to Ramanuja himself.

Vaarththai 70

70. suRRik kiDandhEnO mAlaiyANDAn pOlE
எ0. சுற்றிக் கிடந்தேனோ மாலையாண்டான் போலே

Ramanuja had five main acharyas - Periya Nambi, Thirukkottiyur Nambi, Thirumaalaiyandan, Thiruvaranga Perumal Araiyar and Thirumalai Nambi. Periya Nambi was the one who performed samashrayanam for Ramanuja and is the first acharya for Ramanuja. By his order, Ramanuja learned the rahasyarthas from Thirukkotiyur Nambi. And, based on the order of Thirukkotiyur Nambi, he learned Bhagavad Vishayam (the meanings of Nammazhvar's Thiruvaymozhi pasurams) from Thirumaalaiyandan.

As Thirumaalaiyandan would teach Ramanuja the meanings of Thiruvaymozhi per the teachings of his acharya Swami Alavandar, at some places Ramanuja would propose a different explanation for the pasurams. At one point, Thirumaalaiyandan became upset with the alternate explanations proposed by Ramanuja and told him "These are not the meanings that I have heard from Alavandar. What you are doing is Vishaamitra srushti" and stopped teaching Ramanuja.

When Thirukottiyur Nambi heard that the lessons had stopped, he came to Srirangam and enquired with

Thirumaalaiyandan as to what happened. When Thirumaalaiyandan told him about the alternate meanings suggested by Ramanuja, Thirukkottiyur Nambi told him "I have heard these additional meanings from Alavandar. Ramanuja listening to you is similar to Krishna learning from Sandipa. Ramanuja will not think of any meanings that was not in the mind of Alavandar. Do continue the teachings".

Hearing that, Thirumaalaiyandan became pleased that he was able to hear the meanings of the pasurams that he had missed hearing from Alavandar. He continued the teachings to Ramanuja. This teaching of Thirumaalaiyandan to Ramanuja as per the wishes of Thirukkottiyur Nambi is refered here as *'suRRik kiDaththal'* by Thirukkolur Ammal.

Thirukkolur Ammal is asking "Did I understand the avatara rahasya of Ramanuja and stay with him like Thirumaalaiyandan did".

Another interesting episode where Thirukkolur Ammal refers to an incident in Ramanuja's life to himself.

Vaarththai 71

71. sULuRavu koNDEnO kOTTiyUrAraip pOlE

எ க. சூளுறவு கொண்டேனோ கோட்டியூரரைப் போலே

Periya Nambigal, the acharya of Swami Ramanuja, told Ramanuja that Alavandar had left the task of teaching the rahasyarthas to him with Thirukkotiyur Nambi. He instructed Ramanuja to go to Thirukkottiyur Nambi and learn these esoteric meanings at his divine feet.

Ramanuja walked to Thirukkottiyur from Srirangam and sought Nambi and asked him to teach the meanings. However, Nambi refused to do so right away. He wanted to test Ramanuja and confirm that he was indeed worthy of receiving these great meanings.

Ramanuja made this trip from Srirangam to Thirukkottiyur eighteen times before Nambi was convinced that he could be given the meanings.

Nambi told him to return with his *tridandam* and *pavitram* alone the next time and that he would teach him the meanings. Ramanuja arrived with Mudhaliyandan and Kooraththazhvan and declared them to be equivalent to his *tridandam* and *pavitram*. Nambi took a vow from Ramanuja ('*sULuRavu*') that he would not reveal the meanings of Thirumanthram to anyone other than these two disciples (without testing them).

Later he made Ramanuja come back even without Mudhaliyandan and Kooraththazhvan and taught him the meanings of Charama shloka - once again after taking a vow from him not to teach these meanings to anyone without testing.

Thirukkolur Ammal is asking "Did I demonstrate the strength of mind that Thirukkottiyur Nambi did (in making even a great soul like Ramanuja take a vow before revealing the grand meanings of the sampradhayam)".

---

72. uyirAya peRREnO Umaiyaip pOlE

எ உ. உயிராய பெற்றேனோ ஊமையைப் போலே

In Ramanuja's mutt lived a Srivaishnava who was a mute person. He spent his time in doing whatever services he could provide to Ramanuja. One time, Ramanuja's grace flowed toward him and he took the mute Srivaishnava to a private room. There he closed the door, blessed the Srivaishnava and placed his padhukas on his head. He then signed to the Srivaishnava to take his refuge in those padhukas.

At that time, Kooraththazhvan was watching what was happening through a window. He exclaimed to himself "I am ruined because of my knowledge. If I had been a naive person like this Srivaishnava, I too would have become the target of Ramanuja's grace easily".

The mute Srivaishnava took his refuge at Ramanuja's divine feet from that day forward and considered that as the sole means of survival ('uyirAya').

Thirukkolur Ammal is asking Ramanuja "Did I become the target of your divine grace and receive that which is dearer than life, like the mute Srivaishnava did".

Vaarththai 73

73. uDambai veRuththEnO naRaiyUraraip pOlE

எ ங. உடம்பை வெறுத்தேனோ நறையூரரைப் போலே

Pillai Thirunaraiyur Araiyar was a noble Srivaishnava acharya. One time he and his family went to a place called Thottiyam to worship at the Vedanarayana Perumal temple there. At that time, some antagonists set fire to the temple. Everyone was running away from the temple. Araiyar saw that the divine archa rupam of the Lord was about to catch fire. Unable to tolerate that, he embraced the Lord's form and protected Him. Seeing that, his family including his children too offered their bodies to protect the Lord. In the fire, they all lost their lives.

His devotion and love for the Lord is celebrated by Pillai Lokachariar in his Sri Vachana Bhushanam – *'upEyaththukku iLaiya perumALaiyum periya uDaiyAraiyum piLLai thirunaRaiyUr araiyaraiyum chinthayanthiyaiyum pOlE irukka vENDum'* and *'periya uDaiyArum piLLai thirunaRaiyUr araiyarum uDambai upEkShiththArgaL, chinthayanthikku uDambu thannaDaiyE pOyththadhu'*.

Thirukkolur Ammal is asking "Did I let go of my body for the sake of the Lord, like Pillai Thirunaraiyur Araiyar did".

Vaarththai 74

74. ennaip pOl enREnO uparisaranaip pOlE

எ ச. என்னைப் போல் என்றேனோ உபரிசரனைப் போலே

Uparicharavasu was a king who ruled his kingdom as per dharma. He was famed for his knowledge of dharma and following it sincerely. Due to that, he was blessed by the dharma devata so that he could move about without touching the ground.

One time, during his rule, an argument broke out between rishis and the devas about the sacrificial offering during a yaga. There is a rule in the Vedas about not killing any animal. But, there is also a special rule about being allowed to sacrifice an animal during a yaga. It is said that a goat can be sacrificed after the recitation of specific mantras during a yaga.

Due to the rule that animals should not be killed in general, the rishis created the form of a goat using grains, made it sacred with the mantras and sacrificed it in the yaga. The devas did not accept this sacrifice. They wanted a real animal sacrificed in the yaga. Therefore, the devas and the rishis took their case in front of the king Uparicharavasu and asked him to give a dharmic solution.

Uparicharavasu respected all souls equivalent to his own. His belief was that an animal had as much right to live as he himself did. So, he accepted the argument of the rishis. Angered by this, the devas cursed him that he would touch the ground as he moved about from that time onward.

Another version of the story says that he spoke on the side of the devas. The rishis were angered with him and tried to convince him to speak against dharma. It is said that he corrected the rishis and made them all understand that everyone should live like him following dharma.

In either case, Uparicharavasu comes across as a selfless person.

Thirukkolur Ammal is asking "Did I follow dharma completely and show that all beings are the same as one's self, like Uparicharavasu did".

Vaarththai 75

75. yAn siRiyEn enREnO thirumalai nambiyaip pOlE

எ ரு. யான் சிறியேன் என்றேனோ திருமலை நம்பியைப்
போலே

One of Ramanuja's five acharyas was Thirumalai Nambi. He was Ramanuja's maternal uncle as well. When Ramanuja came to Thirumalai for the first time, his disciples wished him to climb the hills and perform mangalashasanam to the Lord there, as well as see the garden that his disciple Anandazhvan had built there. Ramanuja was hesitant to place his feet on the hills, as it is Adisesha himself who was present in the form of the hills. However, due to the insistence of the disciples he agreed to climb the hills.

As he went up the hills, Thirumalai Nambi came down with the divine water and other prasadams from the Lord and met him on the way.

Ramanuja asked Thirumalai Nambi "O! Swami. For the sake of this small person, did you have to come personally this far? Could you have not send a lesser person?"

Thirumalai Nambi replied "I searched the entire Thirumalai hills and I did not see anyone lower than me".

This is known as *'paraspara nIcha bhAvai:'* - every Srivaishnava considers himself as the lowest person when meeting another Srivaishnava. Azhvar too calls himself *'sIlamillA siRiyEn'*.

Thirukkolur Ammal is saying "Did I show the Srivaishnava quality that Thirumalai Nambi exhibited".

---

76. nIril kudhiththEnO kaNapuraththALaip pOlE

எ சு. நீரில் குதித்தேனோ கணபுரத்தாளைப் போலே

One time an acharya was crossing the Kaveri river in a small round boat. It was late in the night and was very dark. The river was also showing signs of flooding. While in the middle of the river, the boatman told the people in the boat "It appears that we are overloaded and are now at risk of submerging. If one or two people who can swim well jump into the water, then the boat can be saved. Otherwise, we will all drown".

As the water rapids were strong, no one stepped forward. At that time, a lady called Kanapuraththal told the boatman "May you live a hundred years. Please save our acharya who is in this boat and take him safely to the other side". Saying so, she jumped into the water.

Eventually the boat reached the other side. However, the acharya was very sad and said many times "We lost a lady unnecessarily in the water".

Hearing that, Kanapuraththal cried from the river "Swami! I am safe here. I managed to reach a small island. Please do not worry".

The acharya became very happy and with the help of the boatman rescued the lady and brought her to the shore. She fell at the acharya's feet and said "Swami! It was you who came in the form of an island to save me".

He was pleased and told her "If that is your faith, then let it be so".

Thirukkolur Ammal is asking "Did I consider my acharya as everything and was willing to sacrifice myself for the acharya's sake, like Kanapuraththal".

Vaarththai 77

77. nIrOrugam koNDEnO kAsi singganaip pOlE

எ எ. நீரோருகம் கொண்டேனோ காசி சிங்கனைப் போலே

'nIrOrugam' refers to the lotus flower. In the city of Kasi lived a person called Singan. He was an ardent devotee of Sriman Narayana and each day he would go to the ponds in the city and collect lotus flowers and pray to the Lord with them. He was a very adept swimmer.

He developed arrogance about his swimming ability and one time he claimed that he could swim across the flooded ganges back and forth several times. He started doing that when suddenly a quick flood came across and carried him away. He got caught in a whirlpool in the river and he was unable to escape from it. He realized that his arrogance was his undoing and he started praying to the Lord.

He remembered at that time the event of the Lord saving the elephant Gajendra. He prayed "O! Lord. You came to the side of the pond where the elephant sought refuge in You and saved it. In the same way, please save this poor soul as well. I surrender to You completely".

At that time, a sudden gust of wind occured which caused a huge wave in the river. That wave picked up Singan and pulled him out of the whirlpool. It left him safely in the banks of the river.

Realizing the Lord had saved him, Singan prayed to Him with a melted heart. He then continued to worship Him with the lotus flowers without any ego.

Thirukkolur Ammal is asking "Did I pray to Him with lotus flowers every day like Kasi Singan did".

---

78. vAkkinAl venREnO baTTaraip pOlE

எஅ. வாக்கினால் வென்றேனோ பட்டரைப் போலே

Parasara Bhattar was the son of Kooraththazhvan. As a young child, one time he was playing in the banks of Kaveri and saw a procession in which a vidwan called Sarvagna Bhattar was being carried in a palanquin by his disciples. They were crying out his praises as they went along. Parasara Bhattar was upset that in a town where notable scholars such as Ramanuja, Kooraththazhvan, Mudhaliyandan and Embar were residing, such a procession was taking place. So he decided to test this vidwan.

He went to the procession and stopped it. He then held some sand from the river in his hand and challenged Sarvagna Bhattar to give him a count of the sand. Sarvagna Bhattar was stumped and could not reply. Parasara Bhattar then told him "This is a 'fistful of sand'. You cannot even say this much and yet you go around with people crying out your praises".

Sarvagna Bhattar was amazed by this child's prowess. He then enquired about him and found out that he was the son of Kooraththazhvan. He exclaimed "Will the offspring of that which flies just crawl?" and taking Parasara Bhattar on to his palanquin, dropped him off at his home.

At the doorstep, Ponnachchiyar, the wife of Pillai Urangavill Dasar, received the child and heard about the incident. Reciting Dvayam as protection for Parasara Bhattar she took him to his mother Andal and told her "Please do not let this precious child in the streets where evil eyes can fall on him".

Later, after Ramanuja's time, per the instruction of Ramanuja, Parasara Bhattar went to Thirunarayanapuram, where he debated the famed scholar Vedanti and won him over into the Srivaishnava sampradhayam. Vedanti later renounced this world and came to Srirangam to be with his acharya Parasara Bhattar. Named Nanjeeyar by Bhattar, he would later don the acharya peetam of the sampradhayam.

Thirukkolur Ammal is asking "Did I win over opponents with my oratory skills like Parasara Bhattar did".

Vaarththai 79

79. vAyil kaiyiTTEnO embAraip pOlE

எ கூ. வாயில் கையிட்டேனோ எம்பாரைப் போலே

The acharya Embar was known as Govinda Bhattar prior to getting the name Embar. He was a maternal cousin to Ramanuja. In the early part of his life, he had gone on a yatra to Kasi. There, as he was bathing in the river Ganges, a Shiva lingam came into his hand. As such he became a devotee of Shiva, settled in the town of Kalahasti and began maintaining the Shiva temple there.

At that time, due to the request of Ramanuja, Periya Thirumalai Nambi interacted with Embar, corrected him and returned him to the Srivaishnava fold. Embar then moved to Thirumalai and lived with his acharya Periya Thirumalai Nambi and performed services to him. At that time, Ramanuja was also at Thirumalai learning the inner meanings of Sri Ramayanam from Periya Thirumalai Nambi. Therefore, he got opportunities to observe Embar's characteristics.

One of the qualities of a Srivaishnava is feeling empathy for others. This quality was complete in Embar.

One time, Ramanuja noticed that Embar put his hand inside a snake's mouth, then take a bath and continue his services to his acharya.

He asked "O Govinda! What did you do with the snake?"

Embar replied "I noticed that the snake was keeping its tongue out and suffering. When I went near it, I saw that a thorn was stuck in its tongue. So, I pulled the thorn out. The snake then slithered away".

Ramanuja was amazed about his sense of mercy and blessed him.

A snake instills fear in most people and they tend to keep away from it. Yet, in this instance Embar did not fear it and was more worried about its suffering.

Thirukkolur Ammal is asking "Am I capable of showing the level of mercy that Embar did by sticking his hand in a snake's mouth".

Vaarththai 80

80. thOL kATTi vandhEnO baTTaraip pOlE
அ0. தோள் காட்டி வந்தேனோ பட்டரைப் போலே

It is not clear what event is the basis for this Vaarththai from Thirukkolur Ammal. One possibility is as follows.

When Namperumal goes out in a procession in the streets of Srirangam, due to the large crowds, there will be some people in front of the procession who will hit the ground with long belts to clear the crowd. Some times the belt would accidentally hit a devotee.

It is said that one time the belt hit Parasara Bhattar on his shoulder. Bhattars disciples got angry and used harsh words against the person using the belt.

Hearing that, Bhattar told his disciples "They were only doing their duty. There is no mistake in that. Besides, what's wrong in being hit by those in the service of the Lord".

He then told the person who hit him "What you did was correct. When I got hit on one shoulder, I should have offered my other shoulder also to you. That was my mistake and I feel bad about it. Now I am showing you my other shoulder".

The person who had used the leather belt became ashamed and apologized to Bhattar.

It is the quality of a Srivaishnava to show patience and mercy to anyone who errs against them.

Thirukkolur Ammal is asking "Did I show these qualities any time like Bhattar did when he offered his other shoulder".

Vaarththai 81

81. thuRai vERu seydhEnO pagavaraip pOlE

அக. துறை வேறு செய்தேனோ பகவரைப் போலே

In Thiruvayindrapuram lived a Srivaishnava called Villiputhur Bagavar. When he went to the river to perform his daily anushatanams, he would always go to a different part of the river and not to the place where most others would go.

One time the Brahmins who were in their area of the river asked Bagavar "O! Swami. Why do you not perform your anushatanams in our place?"

Bagavar replied "We are Srivaishnavas that follow Swami Ramanuja. We perform these nityanushatanams only as a service to Sriman Narayana. You are brahmins that follow varNashrama dharma. You perform the nityanushtanams as part of your varNa. Therefore, the two of us cannot mix".

Bagavar was either a brahmin who had understood the true nature of the soul or was a sanyasi.

Thirukkolur Ammal is asking "Did I understand the greatness of service and separate from those who follow only the dharma anushatana".

Azhvar Emberumanar Jeeyar Thiruvadigale Sharanam

About the Author

TCA Venkatesan is a descendant of Thirumalai Anandazhvan, a disciple of Bhagavad Ramanuja and one of the 74 simhAsanAdipatis that he created to spread the Srivaishnava Sampradhayam.

He owns and maintains the website http://acharya.org.

Made in the USA
Columbia, SC
17 October 2020

23012339R00089